GW00402193

EXTENDING SCIENCE

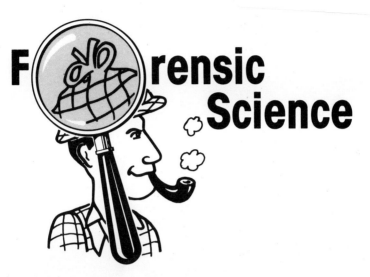

Forensic Science

Selected Topics

T H James BTech MEd

Stanley Thornes (Publishers) Ltd

First published in 1987 by
Stanley Thornes (Publishers) Ltd
Old Station Drive
Leckhampton
CHELTENHAM
GL53 0DN
England

British Library Cataloguing in Publication Data

James, T.
    Forensic science.
    1. Criminal investigation
    I. Title
    363.2'5   HV8073

    ISBN 0–85950–673–8

Typeset by Tech-Set, Gateshead, Tyne & Wear.
Printed and bound in Great Britain by Ebenezer Baylis & Son, Worcester.

CONTENTS

PREFACE

Forensic science can include almost any area of science, and to describe it completely in a book would take many volumes. Although this book can only represent the tip of the iceberg, giving the reader a flavour for the subject, it does nevertheless cover most of the material required for the majority of GCSE courses.

A second difficulty has been that many forensic science courses in schools contain material that is not, strictly speaking, the work of the forensic scientist. My apologies, therefore, to any forensic scientist who reads this book and who is puzzled by the inclusion of certain topics.

I have enjoyed teaching forensic science for many years in school, and have had success with all of the activities used in this book. Considerable care, and common sense, must be exercised in some of the activities however, where hazardous chemicals are involved. The reader is advised to consult one of the many 'Safety' references available, if in doubt.

Terry James
1987

Hazard warning symbols used in this book

Corrosive!

Flammable!

Harmful!

Toxic!

ACKNOWLEDGEMENTS

Many people have assisted in the writing of this book, and I would particularly like to thank:

Gloucestershire Constabulary – Community Services Department, Stroud, and the Photographic Unit, HQ, Cheltenham – for their enthusiastic assistance, and for permission to reproduce the photographs on pp. 17, 18, 28 and 87.

Lion Laboratories Ltd, Barry, South Wales, for providing details of the breath-screening devices, and for the photograph on p. 69.

The *Reading Post* for permission to reproduce the photograph of the Intoximeter in use (p. 70).

The South Western Examination Board for permission to include a selection of examination questions.

Dr T.W. Bentley, University College, Swansea for his assistance and the SERC Mass Spectrometry Centre, University College, Swansea for permission to reproduce the photograph on p. 76.

The Home Office Forensic Science Laboratory, Huntingdon for permission to reproduce the photograph on p. 88.

Matthew Gardner (Highwood School, Nailsworth) whose cartoon characters throughout the book reinforce the sense of fun that this topic can create.

ITN (*News at Ten*) for permission to reproduce the news item on pp. 27–8.

Lyn, Tony, Christopher, David and Richard for their unfailing support during the writing of this book.

INTRODUCTION

Forensic science simply means science which is used in the law courts, the word *forensic* coming from the Latin word *forum*, which is where the Romans used to hold their law court sessions.

A vast number of different types of criminal cases may appear before a court, and, therefore, forensic science can include almost any area of science. However, in general, the work of the forensic science laboratories falls into three main sections. The first (and the largest) section will be staffed by physical scientists (such as chemists, physicists, metallurgists, etc.). The second section will be staffed by biological scientists, concentrating on investigations of offences against the person. The third will be a department dealing with drugs and toxicology. In today's drug culture, much work in forensic science laboratories is concerned with the identification of dangerous drugs and drugs of abuse. There are also specialist departments, including, for example, ballistics, handwriting, photography, etc.

One of the pioneers of forensic science, Edmond Locard of the University of Lyons, identified the basic principle of forensic science: *every contact leaves a trace*, or, more simply, *something always gets left behind!* Forensic science is concerned with the search for, and examination of *contact traces* which result during the commission of all crimes, e.g. murder, assault, theft, burglary, a road accident, etc. Any, or all, of the following may have to be examined:

- Footprints and tyre marks in mud, snow, etc.

- Fingerprints.

- Dents, scratches, or marks, e.g. marks from house-breaking tools; marks left by projecting parts of motor vehicles; teeth marks in food left at the scene of crime by intruders.

- Fibres and fabrics – bits of cloth may be found where an intruder's clothes have caught on something sharp, or on a car which has hit a pedestrian or cyclist.

1

- Bloodstains from minor injuries, e.g. where an intruder cuts himself when breaking in, or on vehicles involved in accidents.

- Soil or mud on clothing or shoes.

- Traces of glass found on clothing or shoes after a break-in.

- Fragments of wood, metal, plastic, etc., broken off when the crime was committed.

- Paint fragments transferred or broken off during a break-in, or in a road accident.

- Oils, dyes, inks – in fact, a whole range of substances can be transferred on to clothing during the committing of a crime.

Most of the above materials would be examined by the forensic chemist and most of this book is devoted to this area of forensic science work.

Fingerprints are also included, though in the UK the forensic scientist has little routine involvement with this area, as most of the work done is carried out by special police departments.

In the first chapter, a brief account of a crime is given, demonstrating, amongst other things, just how easily contact traces may be left behind! Much of the remainder of the book then looks in some detail at how these contact traces are examined by the forensic scientist and his or her colleagues.

<table>
<tr>
<td>

CHAPTER

1

</td>
<td>

THE CRIME

</td>
</tr>
</table>

The white car stopped at the main gate of the Grange, then slowly drove on along the drive. The surface of the drive itself was covered in loose stone chippings, but occasionally the driver of the car felt the back wheels of the car slip a little as it went through a patch of mud where the stone chipping surface had worn thin.

The driver could see the Grange in front of him now. It was all in darkness – his information seemed to be correct, the owners were away for the weekend. No one at home, no dogs, and no alarm systems – a burglar's paradise. He stopped the car by the side of the house, and getting out, he made his way to the french windows.

He stood to the side for a moment, just on the flower border, trying to get a good view of exactly where the inside bolt on the entrance was. He could see it. Using the handle of a large screwdriver he gave the glass pane a sharp knock. It broke instantly, and within a minute he had removed most of the large jagged pieces, enabling him to reach through and slide the bolt. He tried the door; it still would not open – it must be locked as well as bolted. Using the blade of the large screwdriver this time, he carefully slid it between the door and the wooden frame and pulled, in an attempt to lever the door open. At first it felt quite solid, but suddenly it gave way. The door swung open and, losing his balance, he fell backwards. As he picked himself up, he could feel a stinging sensation and he noticed a trickle of blood across the palm of his hand. He had fallen on to some glass from the window that he had carelessly discarded.

The criminal

He entered the darkened room. He pushed his hand against the curtain for a second to dry off the blood, then lit his torch to examine the wound. He wrapped a handkerchief round the hand – he could dress it properly later. He looked around him for a moment and then started searching through a bureau – cash, cheques and credit cards were all that he wanted. Nothing in the bureau; he started searching through the desk drawers. Success, a cashbox! Inside he found notes – mainly £10 notes – about £300 in all. Beneath them was a cheque book.

He searched further for a cheque card; without it the cheque book was of little value to him. No luck! He opened the cheque book, perhaps his luck was in after all? A signed

3

cheque for £5 – a measly £5. He looked at the signature, but decided that he could never forge it in a hundred years! Perhaps though, just perhaps, he could change the £5 into £500; there was room to fill in the extra figures and words and it should be easy enough to find some black ink which was similar to that used on the cheque. A worthwhile evening's work so far, he thought to himself.

The crime

In a split second his elation had changed to blind panic. He could feel the sweat on the palm of his good hand. He had heard a noise; it sounded like a car door slamming at the back of the house. Was it the owner returning early, or the police, or his imagination? He decided not to risk it, and moved quickly towards the window. As he did so he stumbled across a chair. He steadied himself, leaning on the desk for a moment, then continued outside. Voices, he *could* hear voices.

He ran to the car, started the engine, put the car into gear and raced along the drive back towards the main gate. As he approached the gate he stared in his mirror, but nothing was following him yet. This break in concentration, though only for a second, was enough for the car to stray to the side of the drive just as he passed through the gate. He felt a slight thud, and there was a sound of breaking glass as the car struck the gate a glancing blow. His headlamps still worked – it must have been the very front of the wing, a slight dent perhaps and the indicator broken? He put his foot down and drove off at speed. As he did so, he noticed that the oil warning light was glowing on the dashboard of the car. The engine had been losing oil for a few days; he had meant to top it up but kept forgetting.

The following morning he cheerfully made his way to the bank with an amended cheque for £500. It was made out to cash, he was going to the owner's own bank, and he had left the cheque book behind at the Grange. He was hoping that the single cheque that he had removed had not been missed.

As he approached the cashier he again felt nervous. He kept his face partly hidden as he handed over the cheque. He could hear whispered comments behind the counter. Then he saw the policeman coming in through the side entrance, and he turned and ran. Without looking behind him he ran through the side streets, along alleys, then paused for a moment and removed his overcoat. They were looking for a man in a brown overcoat so he furtively threw it into a rubbish skip as he passed, and then casually walked back to his car. As he unlocked the driver's door, he felt a hand on his shoulder.

The arrest

This time he didn't panic – the police couldn't prove anything could they?

EVIDENCE

AT THE SCENE – AFTER THE CRIME!

Whenever the police are called to investigate a crime where several clues have been left, a special police officer called a *Scenes Of Crime Officer* (a SOCO) is called in, who is skilled in examining for fingerprints, and in searching for other clues to send to the forensic scientist for further examination. You may have seen one of these officers on television, examining the scene of some crime, and perhaps picking up certain objects carefully and putting them in plastic bags ready to send to the forensic laboratories.

When the police arrived at the Grange, a very careful examination was made of the house and its grounds. When searching for evidence it is essential to know *where* exactly everything is found, and so either photographs are taken or, alternatively, a careful plan is made of the burgled room and the relevant part of the grounds.

Fingerprints were found at the point of entry, on the bureau, desk, and cashbox; and a full handprint (left hand) was on the surface of the desk. In total, what evidence might the police be able to take to court?

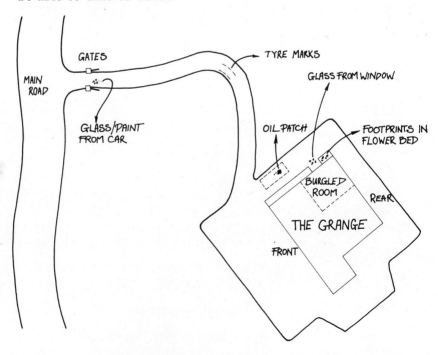

Plan of the grounds
of the Grange

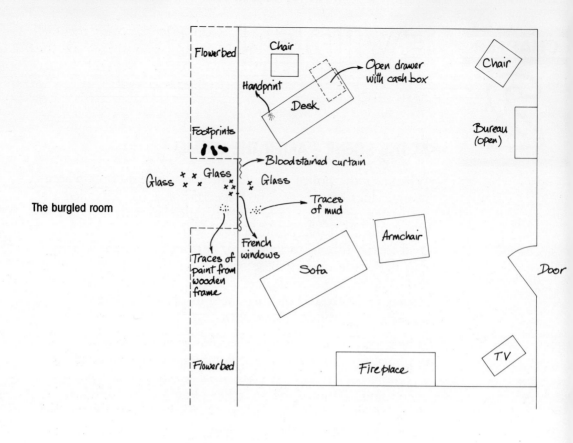

The burgled room

Labels within diagram:
Flower bed
Chair
Open drawer with cash box
Chair
Handprint
Desk
Bureau (Open)
Footprints
Bloodstained curtain
Glass × × Glass × × × Glass
Traces of mud
Armchair
Traces of paint from wooden frame
French windows
Sofa
Door
Flower bed
Fireplace
TV

THE EVIDENCE

Handwritten margin notes:
BLOODSTAINS.
PAINT.
FOOTPRINT:
×
(TYREPRINT.) TYRE TRACKS:
OIL.
GLASS.
FINGERPRINT.
✓ Handprint.
MUD.

- Tyre tracks on the drive (mud).
- Footprints in the flower border.
- Fingerprints on window/bolt, etc., and inside.
- Glass from window on clothes.
- Marks on wooden frame from screwdriver.
- Bloodstains on the floor/broken glass.
- Blood on the curtain.
- Footprints on the patio, and possibly on the carpet inside. Handprint on the desk top (when the intruder stumbled).
- Oil on ground where the car was parked.
- Glass and paint samples at the gate where car collided (some transfer of gate paint to car as well).
- Examination of the cheque – difference in inks.
- Fingerprints on the cheque.

To be able to present so much evidence to the court relies on close cooperation between the scenes of crime officer and the forensic scientist, and a high level of training for both. Carelessness by either of them could result in valuable evidence being destroyed.

WORDFINDER ON EVIDENCE

Try to find the 9 items of evidence against the burglar which are hidden in the word square below. The answers may read across from left to right, or from right to left, or diagonally, or upwards or downwards. Copy the square on to a piece of paper and ring your answers. Do not write on this page. The first one is done for you!

```
S  A  G  F  Q  G  Z  P  O  P  K  F  E  O  O  I  L
S  Z  O  P  Z  A  Z  B  Q  H  T  X  C  H  Y  C  Q
A  D  V  Z  X  S  I  Q  P  O  T  D  C  A  G  T  S
L  E  P  Q  A  T  W  A  C  T  B  B  D  Z  M  J  P
G  Q  X  A  F  Y  E  V  W  O  R  I  G  V  H  I  Y
Z  X  E  J  I  R  X  J  C  F  T  D  G  Y  G  J  O
Q  Z  P  S  B  E  E  F  J  I  I  V  G  H  Q  S  F
R  O  A  T  K  T  L  M  N  T  O  P  H  Q  N  R  C
E  O  P  N  P  R  R  S  Q  U  O  Z  B  I  E  H  T
B  L  K  I  T  A  S  X  G  A  U  C  A  X  E  L  N
Z  L  Y  R  U  C  W  Y  N  F  D  T  T  E  S  M  I
O  D  N  P  U  K  G  J  O  K  S  F  S  W  X  Z  R
P  Z  I  R  K  S  H  O  M  D  F  P  V  T  E  K  P
Q  M  T  E  X  K  T  W  O  N  O  Q  O  Q  F  R  D
R  F  C  G  A  P  Z  O  W  N  R  H  Y  I  Y  P  N
T  S  U  N  R  B  L  S  K  N  I  X  O  B  D  Q  A
S  W  V  I  U  B  T  R  W  O  Q  S  T  V  U  N  H
O  C  N  F  L  N  P  R  Y  M  F  B  M  J  D  C  H
X  T  G  I  O  I  D  Q  S  U  S  G  V  L  P  R  K
S  D  M  F  K  E  H  A  N  D  P  R  G  J  P  O  Z
A  J  L  N  F  R  T  F  I  H  J  T  N  I  A  P  K
```

CHAPTER 3

TOOLS OF THE TRADE

A great deal of modern forensic work now involves the use of very sophisticated equipment, much of which is outside the scope of this book. Nevertheless, two common items of equipment which are as widely used now as in earlier days, are the microscope, and the ultraviolet lamp.

THE MICROSCOPE

The simplest light microscope has only one lens, e.g. the magnifying glass or hand lens. Its magnifying power is generally small, and it can have many imperfections which distort and/or blur the image.

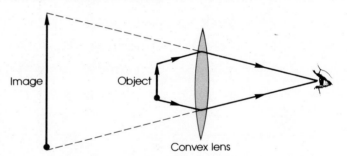

A simple microscope

Image   Object

Convex lens

The convex lens is usually mounted in a frame. In order for it to be used as a magnifier, the lens is placed a short distance from the eye and the object being examined is brought towards the lens until the enlarged image can be clearly seen.

To achieve better quality magnification, we generally use a *compound* microscope, which has a number of lenses.

One group of lenses makes up the *condenser*. This focuses light on the object from below. The light either comes from a lamp or ordinary daylight, and is reflected on to the condenser by a mirror.

A second group of lenses make up the *objective* which produces a magnified image.

Finally, a third set of lenses make up the *eyepiece*, which magnifies the image yet again before we see it.

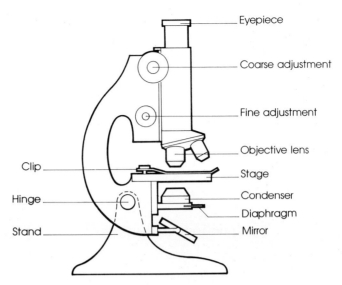

A compound
microscope

Eyepiece

Coarse adjustment

Fine adjustment

Objective lens

Clip

Stage

Hinge

Condenser

Diaphragm

Stand

Mirror

Most student microscopes usually have two or three objectives with different magnifying powers. They can be changed to enable us to see different sizes of image. In routine work, the forensic scientist normally uses a low power microscope, and in the next two activities you will be required to use the low power objective on your student microscope.

ACTIVITY 1

Using the microscope

Caution: Never adjust the mirror so that it is pointing directly at the Sun.

Rotate the nose-piece which holds the objective lenses until the smallest (shortest) one is in position. This is the low power objective lens which gives the least magnification, but is by far the easiest one to use and on most occasions gives a magnification which is adequate for our purposes. Look through the eyepiece and adjust the mirror until you get the brightest light through the eyepiece (try to get the mirror facing a nearby window or light).

Place the object that you want to examine (e.g. human hair, dog hair, strand of cotton or wool – things that look similar when seen with the naked eye) on a slide, and place the slide above the middle of the hole in the stage. Turn the focusing knob, lowering the objective lens until it is about 4 to 5 millimetres above the slide, then look down through the eyepiece and *slowly* screw the objective lens up, turning the focusing knob the opposite way, until the object on the slide appears clearly.

Compare your samples; what do they look like under the microscope? In what ways do they differ in appearance?

9

When the clothes of a suspect are sent to a forensic laboratory for examination, they are sent in sealed packages to ensure that nothing is lost and that no contaminating materials can find their way in. On receipt at the laboratory, they are opened and carefully tipped on to a large table, covered by large clean sheets of paper. Minute fragments of materials which have fallen off the clothing can be carefully brushed up and examined under the microscope. The clothes can then be examined with the naked eye and with a hand lens, followed by a closer examination with a low power microscope. Frequently the most interesting collection of particles is likely to come from the pockets! The fluff at the bottom of the pockets may tell a great deal about the suspect!

Pocket search

Get a sheet of clean white paper: A4 size will do if you are careful. Turn one of your pockets inside out and, using a fairly stiff brush (an old, but clean, toothbrush is ideal), carefully brush the inside of the pocket over the white paper. Be particularly thorough brushing the seams and stitches.

Using the microscope, try to identify the materials that you find. Don't be surprised if you find minute fragments of glass or chips of paint amongst the hairs, fibres, and pieces of grit – this is all quite common! This can also be an interesting way of finding out who the smokers are; tobacco has a strange and very distinctive appearance under the microscope.

To work out what magnification you are using, see what is written on the eyepiece lens and the objective lens. If, for example, they are marked ×10 and ×40 respectively, the total magnification would be 10 × 40 = 400 times.

Although forensic scientists mainly use low power microscopes, occasionally there is a need to look at finer detail. Ordinary microscopes are not much use at magnifications greater than ×450 or so. To examine objects in very fine detail, we need to use an instrument called an *electron microscope*.

As the name suggests, instead of rays of light, a beam of electrons is used to scan the object. When the electrons strike the material under examination, it doesn't just reflect the beam but, in fact, knocks further electrons from the material. These extra electrons can be collected by a detector and produce an image on a screen (like a TV). The image produced is a greatly magnified picture of the material being examined, and magnifications of 200 000 to 250 000 times are not uncommon.

THE ULTRAVIOLET LAMP

When a ray of white light (daylight) passes through a prism, the light splits into a range of colours.

Dispersion of white light

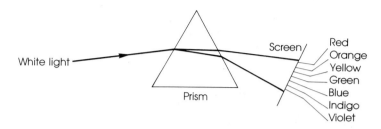

White light — Prism — Screen — Red, Orange, Yellow, Green, Blue, Indigo, Violet

This splitting up of white light is called *dispersion*, and the range of colours produced is called the spectrum. The colours are the same as those that you see in a rainbow, where the raindrops act as prisms and disperse the light in the same way. Two important features are shown by this behaviour:

- White light is a *mixture* of colours.

- Rays of different colours are bent (or refracted) by different amounts as they pass through the prism.

The colours that we see are called the *visible spectrum* because on either side of the visible spectrum there are parts of the electromagnetic spectrum that we *cannot* see: beyond the red is the *infrared* (IR) part of the spectrum, and beyond the violet is the *ultraviolet* (UV) part of the spectrum.

		O	Y	G		I	V	
	R	R	E	R	B	N	I	
INFRARED	E	A	L	E	L	D	O	*ULTRAVIOLET*
	D	N	L	E	U	I	L	
		G	O	N	E	G	E	
		E	W			O	T	

The forensic scientist uses both of these parts of the spectrum in addition to the visible part. UV and IR microscopy have become invaluable tools in the work of the forensic scientist. Infrared radiation is further used in the IR spectrophotometer as described later in the section on breath-testing for alcohol (p. 69).

Ultraviolet radiation causes certain substances to *fluoresce*, i.e. when UV light is shone on to them they give out a greenish/bluish light. Such substances are said to be *fluorescent*. Washing powders usually contain small quantities of a substance which fluoresces with a bluish light when the UV radiation in sunlight falls on to it. This brings out the whiteness of the clothes and helps to mask the natural darkening of an ageing fabric. Some oils also fluoresce under UV light (paper lightly smeared with Vaseline behaves in the same way).

Some materials, e.g. some types of glass, continue to give out light after the UV light has been removed. These substances are said to be *phosphorescent*.

Many substances appear different when looked at under different types of light, and it is often useful to compare the appearance of materials under daylight, UV light, and IR radiation. Many materials can be compared in this way:

- Soils occasionally contain some substances that fluoresce, and comparing the appearance of two soil samples under UV light and in daylight can often add further evidence of matching.

- Samples of inks and dyes, although they may look identical in daylight, often appear very different under UV light and even more different when viewed under IR radiation.

- Using UV light is one way of comparing larger glass samples, though this is of limited use and not a routine part of forensic laboratory procedure.

- Fabrics and fibres may be compared.

- Paint samples may be compared.

- The oil found at the scene of a crime can be compared with oil from a vehicle, or with oil from an item of clothing.

ACTIVITY 3

Looking at oils under UV light

Flammable!

Warning: Never look directly at a UV lamp.
Care! This activity involves the use of petroleum products.

Collect together some samples of various oils, e.g. engine oils of various makes, gearbox oils, household lubricating oils, etc. Taking each one in turn, put one drop on to a piece of filter paper or undyed fabric, labelling each one carefully. When the oils have soaked in, hold each one under the UV lamp. Make a careful note of the colours that you see, in a table.

Name of oil	Appearance in daylight	Appearance under UV

How do the different types and makes of oils differ in appearance? Can UV light be used to distinguish other petroleum products? Repeat the experiment using petrol samples, i.e. different makes and grades of petrol. (**No naked flames!**) Is it possible to compare or identify petrol from different sources?

At one time it was possible to distinguish between oils, etc., using the UV lamp, but nowadays the difference between oils produced by different manufacturers is often minimal, because of greater standardisation.

UV and IR radiation, whether in microscopy, spectrophotometry, or simply from a lamp have become vital tools for the forensic scientist. You will come across them both again in later chapters.

QUESTIONS ON CHAPTER 3

1 White light can be split up into seven other visible colours using the apparatus below.

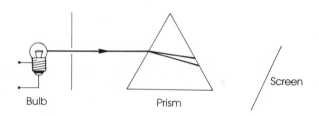

Bulb   Prism   Screen

Apparatus for splitting light

(a) Copy and complete the drawing, showing the rays of light hitting the screen.

(b) The seven colours seen on the screen will be (in order):
red, _____ , _____ , green, _____ , indigo, _____ .

Copy the list and fill in the missing colours.

(c) When the sunlight splits up, some of the rays produced are invisible.
Name 2 types of invisible rays that could be produced by this experiment.

(d) What type of rays are used in:

• The identification of motor oils,

• Heat lamps,

• Sun-tanning beds?

2 Some microscopes are fitted with measuring grids to enable the scientist to estimate the size of the objects that he or she is looking at. The pictures below show three different objects when viewed under such a microscope.

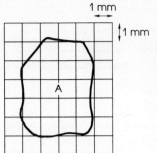
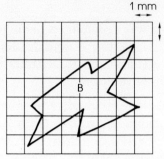
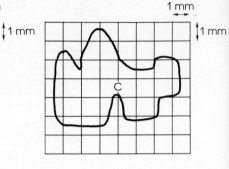

Objects viewed through a microscope

(a) Find the approximate areas of each particle using the pictures above.

- Area of particle A = _____ .
- Area of particle B = _____ .
- Area of particle C = _____ .

(b) Which particle is likely to be picked up most easily on clothing?
Give a reason for your answer.

3 The diagram below shows a compound microscope. Although you are unlikely to be asked to draw one of these, it is important that you know the names of the various parts. Write down the names of the parts of the microscope labelled (a)–(k).

A compound microscope

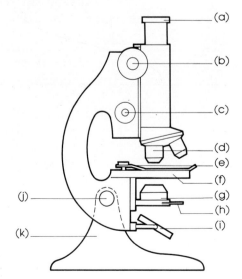

CROSSWORD ON TOOLS OF THE TRADE

Across

4 See 1 *down*
6 See 5 *down*
7 We examine objects under the microscope on these (6)
10 The _____ power of a hand lens is generally small (10)
12 Reflects light on to the condenser lens (6)
16 A set of lenses in the compound microscope (8)
18, 21 _____ _____ radiation cannot be seen with the naked eye (8)
20 A crime involving one of these might provide the forensic scientist with paint and glass to examine (3)
23 Glass block used for splitting up white light (5)
24 7 *across* are placed on this (5)
25 Range of colours produced by splitting white light (8)
26 See 19 *down*

Down

1 and 4 *across* The ultra _____ lamp and compound _____ are widely used in forensic science (6, 10)
2 Magnifying glass or hand _____ (4)
3 An _____ microscope is used to examine objects in very fine detail (8)
5 and 6 *across* Type of microscope most commonly used by the forensic scientist (3, 5)
8 Type of lens which produces a large image (6)
9 Part of a fabric (5)
11 Splitting up of white light (10)
13 Most student microscopes have two or three _____ lenses (9)
14 _____ substances give out a greenish-bluish light when under UV radiation (11)
15 UV radiation can cause certain substances to _____, i.e. they continue to give out light after the UV light has been removed (12)
17 In a microscope, this focuses light on an object from below (9)
19 and 26 *across* Colours of the rainbow (6, 3)
22 Many microscopes have two focusing knobs, i.e. coarse and _____ adjustment (4)

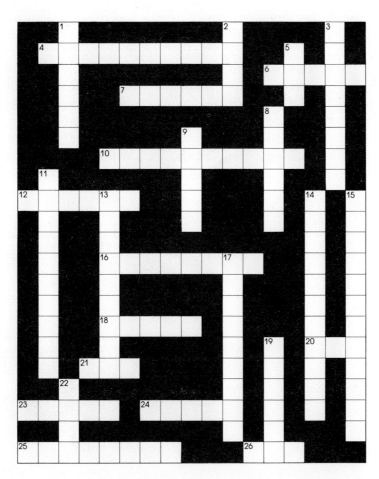

15

FINGERPRINTS

Fingerprints are formed during the fourth and fifth months of life in the womb, and remain unchanged for life (and afterwards – prints have been taken from mummified bodies which were over 2000 years old!).

Fingerprints have been used in the detection of crime since the start of this century. Although they were first described in detail in the 1600s it was not until about 1880 that the idea of using prints for solving crime was seriously considered. It was found that identical prints were not passed on to children from their parents – in fact, each person's fingerprints are unique. In 1898 Sir Edward Henry investigated the patterns in fingerprints, and found that there were three distinct types which he called *arches*, *loops*, and *whorls*.

The fact that no two people, not even identical twins, have the same pattern of arches, loops and whorls means that it is possible to identify someone from the prints left behind on an object. If the prints found at the scene of a crime can be matched with an identical set on record in the police computer files, then the police have a lead to tracing someone who can help them with their enquiries. Of course, they can only do this if the suspect is a convicted criminal whose prints are already on record. However, there is always a chance of matching prints at the scene with those of a suspect detained at a later stage, but it has to be remembered that even a match only proves that the suspect was there, *not* that the suspect committed the crime!

ARCHES, LOOPS AND WHORLS

Three basic types of print patterns have been identified.

A fingerprint may have any of these patterns or, indeed, more than one. If a print contains more than one of these print types it is called a *composite* or *compound* pattern.

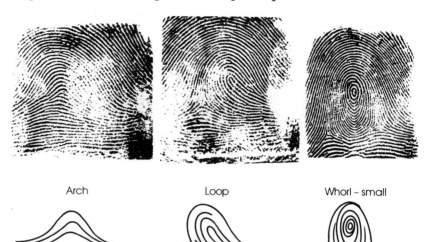

Three basic types of pattern in fingerprints

| Arch | Loop | Whorl – small |

ACTIVITY 4

Looking at your own fingerprints

Roll your fingers, one at a time, on an ink pad (rubbing your fingers across the print of some newspapers has the same effect). Now carefully roll the inked fingers, again one at a time, on a piece of white paper or card marked out as below:

	Little finger	Ring finger	Middle finger	Index finger	Thumb
Left hand					
Right hand					

Look carefully at your prints, using a hand lens if necessary. Are they all of the same pattern? Label the prints on your table: are they arches, loops, whorls, or composites?

Try rubbing chalk across your fingers (or rubbing your fingers across a blackboard!), and pressing hard on to black paper. Cover the prints with Sellotape before they get smudged. Again, examine them carefully. Which method gives the clearer prints?

In practice, the police would normally take the fingerprints twice, i.e. each finger separately, and then the whole hand together, as shown on the 'elimination finger print' chart below.

ELIMINATION FINGER PRINTS

TO BE DESTROYED/RETURNED

NAME....................................   S.O.C.No........................

OFFENCE.................................   OFFICER..........................

ADDRESS.................................   DATE............................

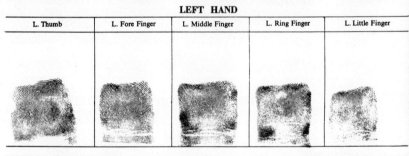

Elimination fingerprints chart

55

ARE YOU A BORN CRIMINAL?

A small-scale survey, carried out by an American James Barr, examined the prints of nearly two hundred men convicted of violent crimes. He noticed that there were many similarities in their fingerprint patterns. When he compared these findings with the prints of 50 ordinary people, it became clear that the violent criminals had more arches and loops, and fewer whorls than the other people. Coincidence? Or can we predict the criminals of tomorrow?

WHAT CAUSES FINGERPRINTS?

The surface of your skin can be covered with many types of substances, e.g. dirt, blood, etc. (or in fact, anything that the skin may have been in contact with), which may be transferred to an object when touched, leaving a print. Even a clean hand may be covered in such substances as water, salts, urea, amino acids, oils, etc., which are naturally secreted from the skin.

Section through the skin

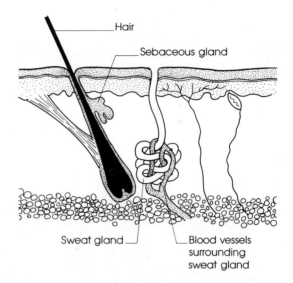

Hair

Sebaceous gland

Sweat gland

Blood vessels surrounding sweat gland

From the sweat gland

Water, salts and urea pass from the blood into the sweat duct and are then secreted through the skin as sweat. As the sweat dries out, so the substances are left on the surface.

From the sebaceous gland

The sebaceous gland makes oil to keep hair soft. Much of the oil produced ends up on the skin's surface.

Small amounts of the substances on the skin are left behind on an object whenever we touch it. Sometimes it will show up clearly as a fingerprint, but on most occasions we need to do something to develop the print (to make it show up more clearly). There are many methods we can use to develop fingerprints: which method we choose will depend on the type of surface where the fingerprint is found, e.g. a non-porous shiny surface; an absorbent surface like paper or cloth; fingerprints in blood; fingerprints on sticky surfaces, etc.

DUSTING FOR FINGERPRINTS

For detecting prints on a non-porous surface, e.g. glossy paper, paint, glass, metal, etc., we would simply dust the area with a suitable powder.

Showing up fingerprints on non-porous surfaces

Care! This activity uses aluminium powder.

Flammable!

Lay some newspaper out flat on the bench – this should make clearing up the surplus powder afterwards easier. Press firmly on some objects – such as glossy paper (Sunday magazines?), a plastic bin liner (black or white), a plastic coffee cup, a glass beaker, etc., – to make a good print. Sprinkle a small amount of powder over the object. If the surface is dark, use a light coloured *fine* powder, e.g. talc or aluminium powder. If the surface is light coloured, use a fine dark powder such as carbon.

The powder sticks to the moist parts of the print which corresponds to the raised parts of the skin. Very gently, brush off the excess powder with a *soft* brush, using the flat of the brush, rather than the tip, to prevent damage to the print. The fingerprint should now be clear enough to be examined and photographed.

FINGERPRINTS ON ABSORBENT SURFACES

Very often it is necessary to detect prints on an absorbent surface like paper or cloth. Fingerprints contain oils from the skin, and these oils can absorb iodine vapour and become coloured, thus showing up clearly.

Showing up fingerprints on absorbent surfaces

Care! This activity involves the use of iodine.
Iodine is a *corrosive, toxic and harmful irritant!*

Take a small piece of filter paper and press your finger firmly on to it to leave a print. Attach a paper clip and cotton to the edge and suspend it in a jam jar, or clear glass coffee jar, to which has been added a few iodine crystals. Replace the airtight lid.

Iodine is a strange substance, in that it quite readily changes from solid crystals to a purple vapour (most substances go from solid to liquid to gas) without going to a liquid stage in between. We call this *sublimination*. After about 10 minutes the print will gradually appear (develop) on the filter paper and be clear enough to examine and photograph.

A fingerprint on filter paper

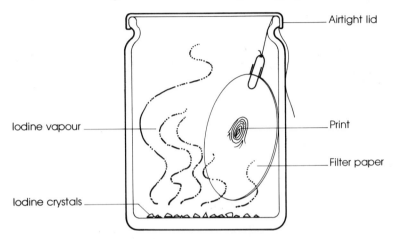

Airtight lid

Iodine vapour

Print

Filter paper

Iodine crystals

If the filter paper is needed for other tests, it could be removed from the jar and left open to the air for an hour or so, and the iodine will sublime again and leave the paper unmarked. If the print is to be kept on the filter paper, it will need to be fixed to prevent it from disappearing. Either:

- Stick Sellotape on the back and front of the print to try to prevent the iodine from escaping.
- Immerse the filter paper into a fixing solution for a few minutes (a solution of calcium chloride, 14 g, and potassium bromide, 50 g, in 120 cm³ water).
- Sprinkle some starch powder on to the print, expose the print to steam *for a second or two*, i.e. hold the filter paper by the spout of a boiling kettle using tongs. A chemical reaction takes place and gives the fingerprints a permanent bright colour.

FINGERPRINTS IN BLOOD

After violent crimes, perhaps the first thing criminals would do is to wipe their hands clean of blood, since even common sense would tell them that they would otherwise leave tell-tale prints. However, even the slightest trace of blood on the fingers will produce prints, which although apparently invisible, can be developed by using a combination of chemicals.

21

Showing up fingerprints in blood

Care!

Corrosive!   *Flammable!*   *Toxic!*

For this work you will need to make up three solutions:

- *Solution 1* 0.2 g of naphthalene black or naphthol blue black (a dye) is dissolved in a mixture of 90 cm³ methanol and 10 cm³ glacial acetic (ethanoic) acid.

- *Solution 2* 10 cm³ of glacial acetic acid mixed with 90 cm³ methanol.

- *Solution 3* 5 cm³ of glacial acetic acid mixed with 95 cm³ of distilled water.

All of these solutions are either *corrosive* or *flammable* or *both*! Care!

Press your finger on to a small piece of fresh liver. Remove most of the blood by making prints on newspaper until the prints become faint. Now make a faint print on a microscope slide. Put the slide into a warm oven (100 °C) for about half an hour, to dry and bake thoroughly. Leave to cool, then, using tweezers, place the slide into a 100 cm³ beaker. Pour in solution 1 to cover the print. The print should become clearer if the solution is carefully swirled around in the beaker.

When it is quite clear, remove the slide with the tweezers and place it in a second empty beaker. Pour in solution 2 to cover the print and swirl the liquid around carefully for two or three minutes. Transfer the slide to another empty beaker and pour in solution 3 to cover the print, swirling around this time for about five minutes.

The fingerprint will now be as clear as it is going to be, so rinse off the slide under the tap and either leave to dry, or carefully place some filter paper over the top of the print to remove excess water. Now that the print has been fixed, it can either be photographed for the records, or kept as it is.

In the case of the careful criminal, who washes the blood from his or her hands then uses rubber gloves while clearing up the rest of the evidence, fingerprints can still be extracted from the inside of the gloves by this method.

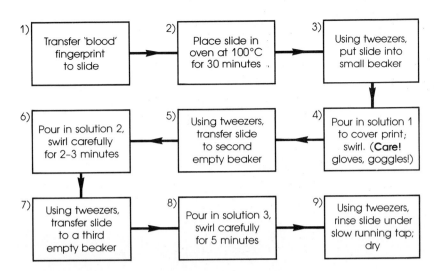

A method for fixing fingerprints

1) Transfer 'blood' fingerprint to slide

2) Place slide in oven at 100°C for 30 minutes

3) Using tweezers, put slide into small beaker

4) Pour in solution 1 to cover print; swirl. (**Care!** gloves, goggles!)

5) Using tweezers, transfer slide to second empty beaker

6) Pour in solution 2, swirl carefully for 2–3 minutes

7) Using tweezers, transfer slide to a third empty beaker

8) Pour in solution 3, swirl carefully for 5 minutes

9) Using tweezers, rinse slide under slow running tap; dry

FINGERPRINTS ON STICKY SURFACES

It may be suspected that there are prints on sticky surfaces, such as on the rim of a wine glass or bottle, on sticky tape, etc. Even though the surface of the glass or bottle is hard and smooth, dusting for prints would be pointless since the powder would stick to everything, and not just the moisture from the print itself. Another chemical method has to be used.

ACTIVITY 8

Showing up fingerprints on sticky surfaces

Care! This activity uses a solution that is *toxic* and *flammable!* In addition, phenol crystals are *corrosive!*

IMPORTANT! TEACHER DEMONSTRATION ONLY

For this work you need to make up a special solution of gentian violet. Add 5 g of gentian violet to 50 cm^3 of industrial alcohol and grind together with 10 g of hydroxybenzene (phenol) in a mortar. Dilute with half a litre of distilled water, stirring continuously. Leave for a day, then filter into a brown glass bottle.

For prints on a glass or bottle, simply immerse it in the gentian violet solution for about 15 to 20 minutes, then wash under the tap. The stickiness is removed, but the print stays behind on the glass, stained a violet colour.

The same gentian violet solution can be used for developing prints on sticky tape. Take a length of clear adhesive tape.

Attach a glass rod at one end (so the tape can be suspended over a beaker), and a nail at the other end – to weigh the tape down (the tape has a habit of tangling up unless it is kept pulled tight). Press your finger firmly on the centre of the sticky tape, leaving a print on the sticky side. Suspend the tape in the gentian violet solution for 10 to 15 minutes.

Remove the tape from the solution, wash under the tap, then carefully dab with filter paper to remove excess water. When placed flat on white card or paper, the prints should be suitable either for photographing or for storage intact.

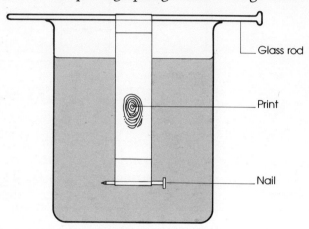

A fingerprint on a sticky surface

Developing fingerprints with ninhydrin

Where there have been difficulties with other methods, ninhydrin could be used. Ninhydrin is a chemical which is sensitive to (or reacts with) substances called *amino acids*, which are also found in sweat. The fingerprints show up in colours varying from pink to red to purple. If, after treatment, the prints are exposed to ammonia, they turn blue and can be clearly photographed. It is a sensitive method in that it can detect prints originally made many years ago. It shouldn't be used on paper with ballpoint ink writing, however, since the solvent in the ninhydrin (propanone) is also a good solvent for the ink!

Using silver nitrate

Silver nitrate reacts with chlorides present in fingerprints to produce silver chloride. When silver chloride is exposed to light it turns dark grey, showing up the print. However, any chlorides present in the background material can cause intense staining and obscure any print found, and because of this silver nitrate is not recommended for use on paper. It is still of value, however, when trying to detect prints on raw wooden surfaces.

Developing fingerprints with silver nitrate

Care!
This activity involves the use of silver nitrate (*corrosive/toxic!*) and methanol (*toxic/flammable!*).

Weigh out 0.2 g of silver nitrate. Dissolve it in 10 cm³ of methanol, stirring continuously. (**Care!** Silver nitrate solution also causes black stains to appear on skin and clothes.) Store the solution in a brown glass bottle until required for use.

Place a fingerprint on a small piece of wood. The wood *must* be untreated. (This method is unsuitable for use on wooden surfaces which have been treated with such things as wax or varnish, or articles which have been wetted.) Pour the silver nitrate solution into a clean dry dish or beaker. With a soft brush, paint the wooden surface with the silver nitrate solution. It is only necessary to wet the surface of the wood: soaking is undesirable. Quickly place the wood in the dark and allow it to dry completely. Place the dry wood under a bright lamp.

Fingerprints should appear as dark images. When the prints are clearly visible, they would normally be photographed. Unless stored in the dark, the background will continue to darken until eventually any prints detected will be obscured.

ANOTHER USE FOR SUPERGLUE?

The other method which has been used with some success in recent years involves the use of Superglue (ethyl or methyl cyanoacrylate). Superglue vapour reacts with water – and possibly some other substances in a print – to produce a white deposit which highlights the pattern of the print. It is not a particularly effective method for developing older prints, or prints on porous surfaces. Some success has been achieved, however, on reasonably fresh prints left on non-porous surfaces. Where the white deposit is formed on a white surface, various dyes or powders can be added to show the print more clearly.

Developing fingerprints with Superglue

IMPORTANT!
TEACHER
DEMONSTRATION
ONLY

Harmful!

Care! Superglue vapour is believed to be non-toxic, but it is, however, irritating to the respiratory system, and will glue skin to skin in seconds. This activity must be carried out in the fume cupboard, and eye protection must be worn. If skin is bonded together, soak the affected area in warm soapy water and gently peel or roll the surfaces apart. Do not pull! If glue gets in the eye, wash thoroughly with warm water and get medical attention.

1) Put a fingerprint on a test tube or small beaker.

2) Place the test tube in a plastic container (e.g. a plastic sandwich box with a sealable lid, or a thick polythene bag – check that there are no leaks).

3) Also place in the box a small beaker one third full of hot water.

4) Finally, add to the box a small dish or porcelain boat. Place 10 to 15 drops of Superglue in the dish and place the lid securely on the plastic box.

5) Carefully place the box in a plastic bowl in the fume cupboard.

6) Place a few 100 g masses on top of the box. Add hot water to the bowl to form a water bath around the plastic box.

7) Leave for half an hour. The reaction between the Superglue vapour and the fingerprint requires heat (hence the hot-water bath) and a high level of humidity (hence the beaker of hot water *inside* the plastic container).

8) After about half an hour, carefully remove the plastic box from the bowl of water. Make sure the fume cupboard fan is on, and then remove the lid from the box to allow the Superglue vapour to escape. Leave for at least 5 minutes before removing and examining the test tube. A white deposit should have built up around the print, outlining the pattern clearly.

It is difficult to lift fingerprints detected by this method, and at this stage they would normally be photographed to produce a permanent record. Many forensic laboratories have quite sophisticated equipment which is used to carry out this procedure, and although the activity described here is rather crude by comparison, the author has obtained quite good results on the majority of occasions.

A use of Superglue

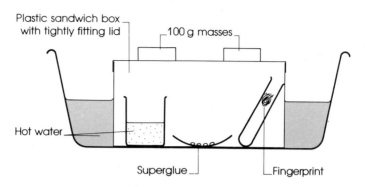

Plastic sandwich box with tightly fitting lid

100 g masses

Hot water

Superglue

Fingerprint

MATCHING FINGERPRINTS

All fingerprints are photographed in order to keep a permanent record. Fingerprints from the scene of a crime are compared with prints on file. To make sorting easier fingerprints are stored by computer under the headings of the main features. This means that instead of having to search through two or three million prints on record manually, the computer does most of the searching and matching and then provides the fingerprint expert with a much smaller number (perhaps only a couple of hundred or so), which he or she will examine personally. The computer would have great difficulty in doing all of the work, since generally the prints from the scene of the crime are not as good as the prints on file.

Nevertheless, only certain police forces in the UK have computer assistance. Nationwide, most of the work on fingerprints is done manually.

STOP PRESS . . .

The Home Office is considering buying a revolutionary computerised fingerprint system based on the latest microtechnology, and it is hoped the new system will save them crucial time – something even the UK fingerprint experts, who are renowned throughout the world, are always short of. The ability to analyse fingerprints is a vital weapon in the armoury of the police.

At present, most police forces rely on manual techniques to help them match a tell-tale print to a possible name. Scotland Yard does have a computer which can match prints, but it is relatively slow and only deals with around 100 000 prints – there are nearly 4 000 000 on file! The Home Office is now considering a nationwide system, which would be much faster and more comprehensive than anything tried before. It is based on the very latest in microtechnology – *transputers* – computers so small they fit on a tiny chip. Each transputer can carry out millions of instructions every second. The system is still being developed, but this is how it works:

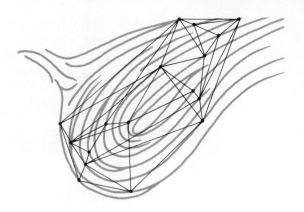

Graph produced by an encoder

An ordinary fingerprint, or part of one, is read by what is called an *encoder*, using six transputers. It breaks down the swirling lines and ridges into a sort of graph showing how far each is from the next, how long the ridges are, and so on.

This information is converted into *binary code*, which is a string of numbers (zeros and ones) which are stored in the computer's memory – it takes less than four seconds! The computer can then scan through its memory at very high speed to match any new print with millions already on file, saving hours of manual labour.

The Home Office haven't made up their mind yet, they want to make sure that a nationwide computer system would be as good as ordinary human skill – something that UK fingerprint experts are internationally acclaimed for.

News at Ten, ITV – 31 July, 1986

In order for fingerprints to be accepted as evidence in court, a print from the scene has to match the print of the subject at 16 points or more, as in the example below.

The prints must match at at least 16 points

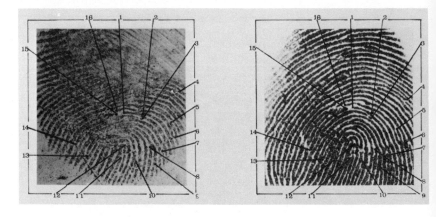

It is normal to start at the centre of the print, working outwards. If the prints are identical in *16* consecutive places, working outwards, then it is a good match. However, if *two or more* prints are found on an item at the scene of a crime, the courts will accept *10* identical points from *each print*.

For all fingerprint analysis work, however, a great deal of specialist training is required in order to carry out the work successfully. Try matching some fingerprints – work in a group – but don't worry if you have some difficulty!

. . . AND WHAT ABOUT OUR SUSPECT BURGLAR?

The burglar in the story didn't panic when the police asked him to 'assist them with their enquiries', he thought they couldn't prove anything. What could they prove so far, just on the basis of fingerprints alone?

- By dusting for fingerprints on the window/bolt, both hard and smooth surfaces, they should be able to establish that he was involved in the break-in.

- By dusting inside, they should find his prints appearing on furniture, cashbox, etc. confirming that he did in fact enter the Grange.

- It should be possible to extract prints from the bloodstains on the curtains where he dabbed his hand dry. Further work carried out on the blood sample, e.g. blood type, etc., could provide additional evidence.

- Fingerprints on cheques left in the cheque book may be found. He probably handled at least one of them when he removed the one that was signed.

- They should find a complete handprint, left when he stumbled by the desk.

- Fingerprints should show up on the cheque handed to the cashier at the bank.

- His fingerprints will be on the car. Later evidence should confirm that the car was present at the scene of the crime (tyre marks, paint, glass, comparison of oil samples from the car and from the ground where the car was parked near the french windows at the Grange).

POSTSCRIPT

A nervous burglar leaves good fingerprints because he sweats when nervous. Someone who is telling lies also sweats more because he or she is subconsciously nervous. This fact can be used in the lie detector machine, which can be accepted as evidence in some countries, but *not* in the UK.

The principle of the lie detector

Try setting up the following circuit.

Hold wires — 0.02 μF — Earphone — Transformer — 9 V — Transistor

Grip each of the wires between two fingers. You should be able to hear a low-pitched tone on the earphone. Wet your fingers by licking them, and hold the wires again. Does the pitch change? When wet, the moisture changes the resistance of your skin which was acting as a resistor in the circuit.

This is how one type of lie detector works. If you tell a lie, the resistance of your skin may change because it becomes damp with sweat.

There are many other more elaborate and accurate methods for lie detection, but all of them rely on the fact that a suspect becomes more nervous when telling a lie. What else happens to the body when a person becomes nervous, apart from sweating?

QUESTIONS ON CHAPTER 4

THINKS

1 There are many ways of revealing fingerprints. They depend on the type of print and the surface that it lies on. Copy and complete the following sentences using some of the words given in the list.
acetone (propanone), ammonia, carbon, Fry's reagent, gentian violet, ninhydrin, talc, iodine.

(a) _Talc_ is used on hard, smooth, dark surfaces.

(b) Fine _carbon_ powder is used for prints on hard, smooth, light-coloured surfaces.

(c) For rough absorbent surfaces like cloth or paper, the print is exposed to _iodine_ vapour. This dissolves in the small droplets of oil in the print and the fingerprint is developed.

(d) _ninhydrin_, which reacts with amino acids, can be used to develop fingerprints. This is sprayed on to the fingerprint which turns blue when exposed to _ammonia_

(e) Prints on sticky surfaces such as wine glasses can be developed with a solution of _____ in phenol and alcohol.

gentian violet

2 Explain the following things.

(a) Good fingerprints will not be obtained if a stick of white chalk is rubbed over a smooth dark surface that a thief has touched.

(b) A nervous thief will leave better fingerprints than a calm one.

(c) Black powder is not good for detecting fingerprints on Sellotape.

3 The sentences below have words missing from them. Choose a word to fill the gap from the list of words that follows. Each word will be used only once and some will not be used at all. Copy and complete the sentences.

fat   flour   George   Henry   iodine
salts   sebaceous   soot   sugar   urea

(a) The man who first introduced fingerprinting into this country was called Sir Edward _Henry_.

(b) The chemicals on your fingers that make fingerprints come from sweat glands and _sebaceous_ glands.

(c) Sweat contains _salts_ and _urea_.

(d) Fingerprints may be made clearer by dusting them with a fine white power such as _talc/flour_.

(e) Fingerprints on a white surface could be dusted with _soot_.

4 (a) Three fingerprints are shown below.

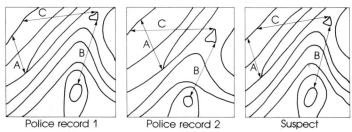

Police record 1   Police record 2   Suspect

On each print, make the measurements shown and record them in a table like the one below. One measurement has been done for you as an example.

Measurement	Record 1	Record 2	Suspect
A	10 mm		
B			
C			

Handwritten margin notes:

3 types of pattern in finger prints

arches/loops/whorls or composite

have to match at at least 16 points

milk/white paper

chalk/black paper

talc

powder ? on carbon } non-porous paper etc

iodine — absorbs oils — on absorbent surfaces

starch powder

Three fingerprints

ninhydrin – for amino acids + ammonia in sweat.

gentian violet M

sticky surfaces.

31

(b) Which print from the police records is most likely to be that of the thief?

(c) How many measurements must a forensic scientist make to prove that two fingerprints are the same?

(c) In some countries, fingerprints are used instead of signatures. Can you give two reasons for this?

CROSSWORD ON FINGERPRINTS

Across

1 He investigated the patterns in fingerprints (5)
2 Type of fingerprint pattern (6)
6 Type of fingerprint pattern (5)
8 and 2 *down*   Substances found on the skin's surface (4, 10)
10 Fine white powder used for detecting prints (4)
11 Used to detect prints on absorbent surfaces (6)
13 11 *across* does this when warmed (8)

14 See 9 *down*
16 Fine black powder used for detecting prints on a light smooth surface (6)
17 All fingerprints are _____ in order to keep a permanent record (12)
18 A chemical which is sensitive to amino acids (9)

Down

1 The air needs to be _____ when developing prints with Superglue (5)

2 See 8 *across*
3 Fingerprint containing more than one type of pattern (9)
4 Type of fingerprint pattern (6)
5 and 7 *down*   Glands in the skin (5, 9)
9 and 14 *across*   A dye used when detecting prints in blood (11, 5)
12 and 13 *down*   Used for developing prints on a raw wooden surface (7, 6)
15 _____ violet is used when looking for prints on sticky surfaces (7)

5

CASTS

LOOKING AT CASTS

... The burglar stood to the side of the window for a moment, just on the flower border, trying to get a good view of exactly where the bolt was ...

The footprint in the flowerbed is a valuable clue in many detective stories, and indeed, a good clear footprint can provide a great deal of information. People all walk differently and wear out the soles and heels of their shoes in their own unique way.

However, if footprints are to be used as evidence in court, a permanent record has to be made which can be produced in court, in order to make it easier for the jury to understand exactly what is being said. A permanent record would have to be kept anyway, even after the trial, in case the convicted man should appeal at a later date.

This isn't confined, of course, just to footprints. Any impression or dent may provide useful information at a later date: tyre marks are another very important source of evidence. It is vital, therefore, that permanent records are made before the prints get spoiled. One of the most commonly used methods of preserving marks is to make a *cast*. This is done by pouring a special liquid into the mark or print. The liquid dries hard, and when lifted away and cleaned, shows a replica of whatever made the original mark or print. The choice of materials used for making the cast will depend on the conditions under which it is to be made. For a footprint or tyre mark at the scene of a crime, plaster of Paris may be used since it is cheap and easy to prepare.

ACTIVITY 12

Making plaster casts of footprints/tyre marks

Find or make a footprint or tyre mark in damp ground. Use a bowl or tray of soil inside, if necessary. Taking care not to disturb the print, use a thin strip of card (or Plasticine) to make a border around the print to contain the plaster of Paris when it is poured in.

Take about 7 parts of plaster of Paris and 4 parts of water, by volume, and mix thoroughly. Try to make sure that all the air bubbles are removed. When the mixture has the consistency of thick cream, pour immediately into the mould. A piece of cloth, or a few lengths of wooden splints, could be laid across to strengthen the final cast.

Leave to dry, preferably overnight. (NB Clean the container that you used for mixing the plaster **now**, before it sets hard.) When the cast is set hard lift it carefully and wash it gently under the tap. Use a soft brush to remove dirt particles if necessary.

When a burglar uses a jemmy or screwdriver to force open a door or window, scratch marks are made on the wood or metal frame. They may not be very deep, and it could well be that they are on an upright part of the frame. Obviously, if plaster of Paris were used it would simply run out. We need to use something like Plasticine which we can push into the indentation. However, Plasticine always remains soft and a cast made of this material could easily be spoiled at a later time. Very often dental composition is used instead.

Making casts of scratches on metal (dental composition)

Using the blade of a screwdriver, make a shallow dent in a piece of lead. Place some dental composition in hot water. Leave until it is soft but not sticky. Roll into a sausage shape, check that there are no obvious marks on its surface, and press the composition firmly into the dent on the lead, using fingers and thumb. Leave the composition to cool and harden and then carefully remove it. Compare the cast with the original screwdriver, using a hand lens if necessary. Can you pick out the same fine detail on both?

Very often the police will need to make casts on metal which will show up very fine detail indeed. A method has been found that will record marks only about 1/500 000 cm wide! It uses the familiar materials *carbon* and *sulphur*. Carbon can be found in various forms, but here we use *graphite*, a black solid used in pencils. Sulphur is a yellow solid, also found in different forms (called *allotropes*).

Looking at scratches on metal (sulphur and carbon)

Find a piece of metal that is scratched (or make some marks yourself – aluminium is ideal, it is a soft metal which is easily scratched). Roll some Plasticine into a strip, put it around the scratch on the metal to form a ring.

Mix together some powdered sulphur (8 spatula measures) and powdered graphite (2 spatula measures) in a tin lid or crucible. When mixed thoroughly, put the tin lid on to a pre-heated sand bath (this allows a more gradual heating up and minimises the risk of any sulphur vapour catching fire, producing poisonous sulphur dioxide fumes).

Continue heating the sand bath until the mixture melts. Using tongs, pour the molten mixture quickly into the Plasticine mould, and leave to cool. Remove the Plasticine, and lift off the cast. How well have the scratches shown up? You may even notice other marks on the edge of the cast from your fingerprints when you handled the Plasticine.

NB

You will have noticed that the mixture of sulphur and graphite melts easily and solidifies very quickly to make detailed casts. The fact that it does solidify so rapidly also makes it an ideal mixture to use for casting in wet ground, where plaster of Paris would have difficulty in setting. A similar method is used for making casts in snow!

In addition to being used in identifying a suspect and/or a vehicle by straightforward matching, footprints and tyre marks can also provide a wealth of information *about* the person or vehicle. Some information can be easily obtained, e.g. measuring the footprint to establish shoe size.

What other information could be deduced? Would it be possible to tell, for example, whether the person leaving the footprints was running, walking, carrying a heavy load in front, carrying a heavy load on his back, walking backwards, etc.?

Connection between British shoe size and length of print

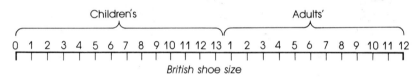

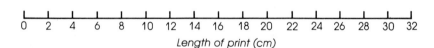

What were they doing?

Try walking, running, carrying loads, etc., through the sandpit on the sports field (or any suitable damp ground). Look at the prints carefully and try to decide whether a whole print has been left or whether just the heel or the sole has made a mark. Is it deeper at the front than at the back? What is the distance between the prints?

Now get someone else to make some prints without your seeing. Using the information that you have found out for yourself, can you decide what activity they were doing?

Tyre tracks also can give further information, for example, speed and direction of a vehicle. Again the work can be complex, but Activity 16 should allow you to get some idea of what is involved.

ACTIVITY 16

Bicycle tracks

How fast were they going?

You will need a bicycle (make sure the tyres have sufficient tread on them!), and a patch of muddy ground. Ride the bicycle across the muddy ground slowly, then turn it round and ride back at the same speed. Compare the two sets of tracks carefully, looking particularly at the tops of the ridges of the tracks – are they straight up or pulled to one side?

You should be able to see part of the tread pointing in a particular direction, indicating the direction in which you were riding.

Repeat, riding faster across the muddy patch. What difference in the print does riding faster make?

HOW DO WE CHOOSE A CASTING MATERIAL?

There are many substances which could be used for casting in addition to those mentioned previously. Ideally, a casting material *should*:

- Be cheap.
- Be easy to prepare and use, even under poor weather conditions, or in remote places.
- Set quickly.
- Be able to make a detailed and accurate cast of the mark/print.

A casting material *should not*:

- Shrink or expand after it has set.
- Stick to the mark or print.
- Damage the mark or print when removed.

Since no one substance has yet been found which is suitable for all occasions, a choice has to be made from the available substances. Which casting material we choose depends on:

- The size of the mark or print; if large, e.g. several footprints, the material will need to be cheap.

- What material the print is in, e.g. prints/marks in soil, scratches on metal, dents in wood, etc.

- Whether we need to pick up the *fine* detail in the mark.

- Whether the print or mark is on a flat surface or a vertical one.

- Whether the print or mark needs to be kept undisturbed after casting, e.g. does it matter if it is destroyed?

Activities 12, 13 and 14 (pp. 33–4) cover the three main types of casting materials currently in popular use.

QUESTIONS ON CHAPTER 5

1 When the police need to make casts of scratches on metal, they use a mixture of graphite and sulphur.
  (a) Copy and complete the following sentences. Use words from the following list:

black	carbon	dissolves	evaporates	grey
melts	quickly	sand	slowly	silicon
white	yellow			

  Sulphur is a _____ solid. Graphite is a _____ solid, and is a form of _____. The mixture _____ easily and solidifies _____.

  (b) Give two advantages of using the carbon/sulphur mixture compared with using plaster of Paris.

2 Read the following paragraph carefully.

  During the early morning it had rained heavily, but by 10.00 a.m. it had stopped, and it stayed dry until 12.30 p.m. There were two light showers between 12.30 p.m. and 1.30 p.m. and then it remained dry until the crime was discovered at 3.20 p.m. Footprints and tyre tracks were found at the scene of the crime. They were clear prints, having just a little water in them.

  (a) What time of day do you think the crime was committed? Give a reason for your answer.

  (b) What substance could be used to make a cast of the footprints?

  (c) Name *one* other common use for this substance.

  (d) From the list on the next page select the things which would make good casts using the substance you have named.

dog's footprint   marks on a metal window frame
show print in the snow   scratches on a stone floor
tyre print in wet ground

3 Look at this bicycle tyre tread left in some soil.

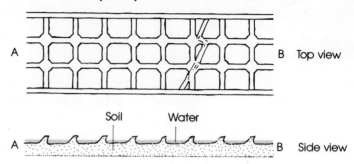

Bicycle tyre tread

(a) By looking at the track, what can you say about the tyre that may help identify it when compared with similar tyres?

(b) What can you say about the direction the bike was moving in?

4 A footprint has been found in a flowerbed. The soil in the bed is mainly clay and it has been raining all night.

A forensic scientist wants to make a plaster cast of the print so that he can examine it in the laboratory. The list that follows contains the things that he must do – but they are all jumbled up.

A   Pour plaster of Paris mixture into the footprint.
B   Drain the water out of the footprint.
C   Make a plaster of Paris mixture.
D   Allow the plaster of Paris to set.
E   Press the plaster cast into a box of damp sand.
F   Lift the cast out of the flowerbed.

Rearrange A to F, and copy them out, putting the six stages into the correct order.

SOIL

When the burglar stood in the flowerbed, in addition to leaving footprints, some soil will also have been transferred to his shoes. The forensic scientist, by matching soil on the shoes with soil from the scene of the crime, can obtain even more evidence for the prosecution (or in some cases, of course, for the defence). Unfortunately, evidence from soil comparisons tends not to carry as much weight as, say, fingerprints or casts, since soils a few feet away from each other can vary quite considerably. It is necessary, therefore, to determine not only that the soil from the suspect's shoes matches the soil in the flowerbed, but also that it matches the soil in the *same part* of the flowerbed as the footprints were found. Obviously the more tests the forensic scientist carries out on the soils, the more likely he or she is to make a fair and accurate comparison.

Soil is made up of small pieces of rock varying in size from minute dust-like particles to much larger lumps. Mixed with this is normally found *humus* (rotting plants and animals), water and a variety of other chemical substances. Soils from different areas (or even different parts of the same area) may vary quite considerably in the size of particles they have, and the amount of humus, water, chemical substances, etc., they contain. The result is that soils from different places can *look* very different. In the table below you can see that just having small amounts of various substances present can make the soil look a quite distinctive colour.

Substances present in soil	*Colour of soil sample*
Silica or lime	White or light grey soils
Humus (rotting plants, etc.)	Black or dark grey
Iron compounds	Brown, red, or yellow

Comparing two soil samples

Ask someone to get you two soil samples, soil A and soil B. They may be from the same place, or from different places – don't ask, it's up to you to find out! (Keep some samples of soils A and B for later activities.)

Examine the soils closely, using a hand lens if necessary. Do they look the same colour? (**Care!** If the soils are of different dampness, the damp soil will look darker than the drier one.) Are the particles roughly the same size or obviously different? Is there much evidence of humus, leaves, roots, etc.? Hold the soil sample under an ultraviolet lamp. Do the samples look different in any way?

To avoid confusion when comparing results of your activities at a later stage, it may help to record *all* of your observations in a table.

Observations	Soil A	Soil B

Some soils are capable of holding on to more water than others, due to the differences in the sizes of the particles in them. Soils can fall into three main categories: sandy soils, clay soils, and loam.

Sandy soils

As the name suggests, these contain a high proportion of sand particles. These particles can vary in size and shape, but somewhere in the region of 0.15 to 0.30 millimetres diameter might be considered typical. These are relatively large particles (compared with clay), and the air spaces between them are also quite large. This means that rainwater can easily drain through sandy soil, and it therefore retains very little water.

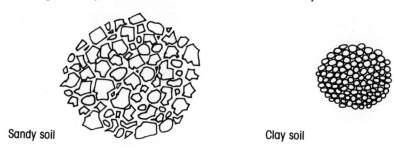

Sandy soil   Clay soil

Clay soils

These are made up of much smaller particles (about 1000 times smaller than sand particles). The air gaps between the clay particles are also smaller and rainwater has great difficulty in draining through. Clay soil, therefore, tends to retain water and is usually quite sticky.

Loam

This is a soil which really appears to be midway between the extremes of sand and clay, and contains much more humus.

The differences in water retention of soil can be used to compare samples.

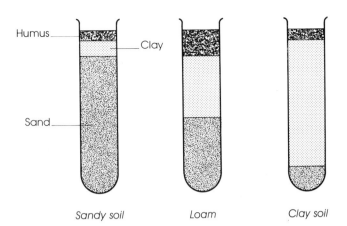

Soil samples

Humus
Clay
Sand

Sandy soil   Loam   Clay soil

Water content of soil

Take about 5 g of soil samples A and B (Activity 17) and accurately weigh each in separate evaporating basins.

Soil A   Mass of basin = _____ g
          Mass of basin plus soil A = _____ g
          Mass of soil A = _____ g
Soil B   Mass of basin = _____ g
          Mass of basin plus soil B = _____ g
          Mass of soil B = _____ g

Each evaporating basin is then placed on a sand bath, and heated gently for about twenty minutes. **Care!** You are trying to evaporate off the water, but *not* burn the soil. Allow the soil and dishes to cool, then reweigh each basin.

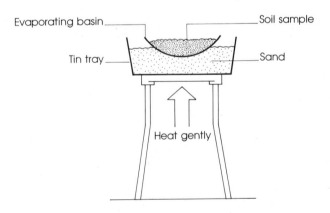

Evaporating basin   Soil sample

Tin tray   Sand

Heat gently

Do not burn the soil!

After heating

Soil A   Mass of basin plus soil A = _____ g
          Mass of soil A = _____ g
Soil B   Mass of basin plus soil B = _____ g
          Mass of soil B = _____ g

The difference in the masses of soil before and after heating must be due to the water that has evaporated. The percentage of water in the soil must be:

$$\frac{\text{Difference in mass before and after heating}}{\text{Mass of soil before heating}} \times 100$$

Work out the percentage of water in soil A and soil B.

Are the percentage water values roughly equal for soils A and B, or significantly different? Also at this stage, compare the appearance of the soil samples. Have either changed in colour, etc.? Complete the table to summarise your observations.

Test	Soil A	Soil B
% water		
Appearance in daylight		
Appearance under UV		

Keep the dried samples of A and B for the next activity.

As mentioned previously, different soils may contain differing amounts of humus. Since humus is an organic substance it can be changed into carbon dioxide and water by strong heating. The loss in mass of the soil when strongly heated is, therefore equal (approximately) to the amount of humus originally present. In addition, some ash will remain, which may be coloured by any minerals present.

ACTIVITY 19

Humus in soil

Take the samples of soil A and soil B from Activity 18. Accurately weigh the sample of soil A in an evaporating basin. Place over a tripod and gauze, and heat strongly for ten minutes. Then heat from above for a further five minutes. Allow to cool, and then reweigh the basin and its contents. Make a careful note of all your weighings.

Soil A

Before burning	Mass of basin = _____ g	
	Mass of basin plus soil A = _____ g	
	Mass of soil A = _____ g	
After burning	Mass of basin plus soil = _____ g	
	Mass of soil A = _____ g	

Therefore, loss in mass = _____ g, i.e. this is the amount of humus that was present in soil A.

The percentage of humus present is:

$$\frac{\text{Difference in mass before and after burning}}{\text{Mass of soil before burning}} \times 100$$

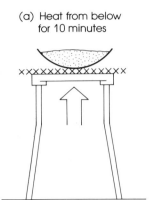

(a) Heat from below for 10 minutes

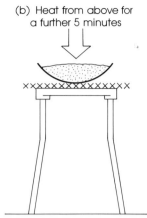

(b) Heat from above for a further 5 minutes

Heating the soil

Has the soil changed in appearance? Examine the soil sample in ordinary daylight and under UV light if possible (refer back to Activity 3, p. 12 before using the UV lamp). Record your observations in the table.

Now repeat the whole activity, this time using a sample of soil B.

Test	Soil A	Soil B
% humus		
Appearance in daylight		
Appearance under UV light		

pH – ARE SOIL SAMPLES ACIDIC, ALKALINE, OR NEUTRAL?

Some substances in a soil sample may dissolve in water to form acidic, alkaline or neutral solutions. We can use an indicator to show us which it is. Universal Indicator is used in preference to many others because it not only tells us whether a substance is acidic, alkaline, or neutral, but also gives us information about the strength of the acid/alkali. Universal Indicator has a range of colours, each corresponding to different strengths of acid/alkali.

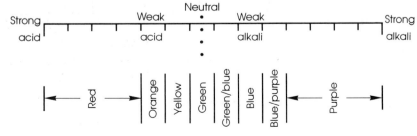

pH scale using Universal Indicator

Many people have difficulty in describing colours, so we have a standard colour chart on which each colour is given a number (called the *pH*).

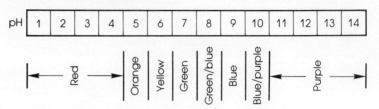

pH numbers

An *acid* solution would give a pH of less than 7.

A *neutral* solution would give a pH of exactly 7.

An *alkaline* solution would give a pH of greater than 7. (NB Most soils generally fall in the range of pH 3.5 to 8.5)

Finding the pH is, thus, yet another simple test which can be carried out to compare soil samples

pH of soil

The pH of soil samples can be found easily using method 1, or if available using *barium sulphate tubes* which give a more accurate pH value (method 2).

Method 1

Using soil samples A and B from Activity 18, take each in turn and put about three spatula measures of each into separate test tubes. Half fill each test tube with distilled water, fit a cork or bung and shake well. Carefully filter each muddy solution, and test the clear solution that comes through each filter (the *filtrate*) with Universal Indicator. Record its colour in your results table, and match the colour against the standard colour chart to find the pH. Is it acidic, alkaline or neutral?

	Colour	*pH*	*Acid/alkali/neutral*
Soil A			
Soil B			

Method 2

A barium sulphate tube is a glass tube about 20 cm long, stoppered at each end.

Place the stopper in the bottom of the tube and add about 5 cm³ of soil. Add distilled water up to the mark (b), then add Universal Indicator up to mark (a). Add one spatula measure of barium sulphate (this helps the liquid to clear

A barium sulphate
tube (Method 2)

faster), stopper the top of the tube and shake or invert the tube until the contents are well mixed. Leave in a test tube rack until the contents have settled and a clear liquid is obtained. Match the colour of this clear liquid against the standard colour chart, and make a note of the pH. Is the soil sample acidic, alkaline or neutral?

For more accurate measurements, an electrical instrument called a *pH meter* can be used.

Soil particles vary considerably in size and the proportions of different sizes present in two soil samples can be used to compare them. The main types of particles present in soil samples are given in the table below.

Type of particle	Particle size (diameter in mm)
Gravel	more than 2
Coarse sand	2.0–0.2
Fine sand	0.2–0.02
Silt	0.02–0.002
Clay	less than 0.002

The simplest method to examine the sizes of particles in a soil sample is to dry the soil, break up any obvious large lumps, then pass it through a set of sieves covering a wide range of sizes. For example, first the soil can be shaken on to a sieve with large holes; small particles pass through, larger particles are trapped on the sieve. If this is done using a large number of sieves, getting successively smaller each time, the soil trapped on each sieve can be weighed. We can then work out the proportion of gravel, sand, silt, etc., in each soil sample. Some typical results are shown below.

Soil analysis graph

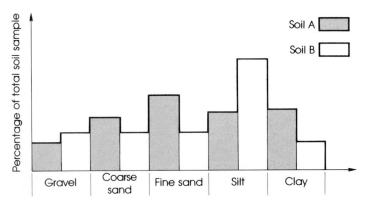

These two soil samples are obviously different. This is not a particularly accurate method, however, since many of the smaller particles still remain clumped together. More sophisticated methods are generally used, but these are outside the scope of this book.

QUESTIONS ON CHAPTER 6

1 A sample of soil was taken from a suspect's shoe for analysis. Here are some of the details from the forensic scientist's note book for you to study

> *Examination of soil under microscope*
>
> A   Particles seen: yellow and red specks
>   white lumps
>   small pieces of grit
>
> B   Sketch of particles seen under microscope:

Grit particles

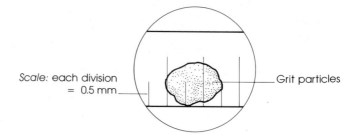

Scale: each division = 0.5 mm —⎯   Grit particles

> C   Action of Universal Indicator on soil: pH value 9.

Now answer these questions:

(a) The suspect was thought to have been on a building site.
    Suggest what the particles and lumps might have been.
    yellow and red particles: _____
    white lumps: _____

(b) What was the diameter of the lump of grit?

(c) Was the soil acid or alkaline?

(d) What substance, found on a building site, might have given the soil this pH value?

2 (a) One way to compare different soil samples is to dry them to see how much water they contain. The results of such an experiment are shown below.

Before heating: Mass of dish = 42 g
                    Mass of dish and soil = 86 g
After heating: Mass of dish and soil = 62 g

- What is the mass of soil before heating?

- What is the mass of soil after heating?

- How much water must have been present in the original soil sample?

(b) The table below shows the rate at which two soil samples lose mass when they are heated gently to dry them.

Time (minutes)	0	5	10	15	20	25	30
Mass of soil X (g)	70	56	51	49	48	48	48
Mass of soil Y (g)	70	51	47	43	41	39	39

Plot these results on a graph. Draw your axes as shown below.

Loss of mass when soil samples are heated

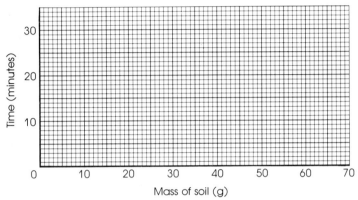

(c) How long did it take to dry soil X?

(d) What mass of water was there in soil Y?

(e) Which soil is likely to be a clay type? Give a reason for your answer.

3 A load of soil was tipped near a football pitch ready to carry out some repair work. Overnight it disappeared. When the police made an investigation the following day, they found similar looking soil lying in the drives of two houses. Soil samples from the field and from the two houses were taken away for comparison. The results are shown below.

Observation	Soil from field	Soil from house 1	Soil from house 2
Colour	brown/black	brown/black	brown/black
Particle size	small/medium	small/medium	small/medium
Plants found	grass	grass	grass
Dampness (% moisture)	7.2%	8.3%	7.9%
pH of soil	8	6	4

Look carefully at the results, then answer the following questions.

(a) Do the results provide any clues as to where the missing soil has gone?
Explain your answer.

(b) Name two other tests that could provide more evidence.

WORDFINDER FOR SOIL

Try to find the answers to the following questions in the wordsquare below. The answers may read across from left to right, or from right to left, or diagonally, or upwards or downwards. Copy the square on to a piece of paper and ring your answers. Do not write on this page!

Use as cl.

1 These chemicals may be found in light grey soils (two answers)
2 Iron compounds may turn soil this colour
3 A mixture of sand/clay; contains a lot of humus
4 Used for testing pH of soil (two words)
5 Used to examine the sizes of soil particles
x 6 Barium sulphate helps muddy water to _____ faster
7 The particles in sandy soil are generally _____ than those in a clay soil
8 The air spaces between clay particles tend to be quite _____ compared with those in sandy or loam soils
9 _____ is made up of rotting vegetation (plants) and animals

9. which type of soil dries quickly
10   is likely to be heavy + wet.

```
R E L T T E S A F T O A B G L A C
I P M L R E S A I S F E G L B E J
S N E G O T O D A I N E A W O H A
K K A M C U Q C I U D M W B A C E
P A L D I F I G F E S U O G U A W
P Y O X U L R O I L E S S S H O O
A R M N I N S A N O W I C M A O L
L W C S A F E T D Y I N U I A R L
A D O T J H A E I L A O B O R A E
R E F S S I D L C W S A F E T B Y
G C O H G P E A A I D S E S T D A
E P A R T O F S T R N E H Y I S O
R N I M P O R R O T A N V T F H G
F C V I D R D E R T U E G E T I B
P O S B U T V V O T C O P R I U Q
W U U D O A P I G N O S F O R S T
C A S G E E C N T I F A G A U Q U
W A I U F O S U M U H P I C K G B
R A E L C U A I R T A G U C H E R
```

CHAPTER 7

PAINT AND GLASS

Investigation of paint and glass samples makes up a high proportion of the work of the forensic scientist. In the crime described earlier in the book, the burglar would probably have collected some paint flakes and glass fragments on his clothes as he broke the window to gain entry to the house. Glass from the car would have been left by the gate posts when he collided with them as he left the scene of the crime. Paint from the car would have been transferred to the gate, and that from the gate may well have left traces on the car when the collision took place.

A small-scale survey carried out in 1966 by the Home Office Central Research Establishment tried to find out how common paint and glass samples were on clothing. They chose a hundred people at random, and brushed down their clothes in an attempt to work out the possibility of a particular type of paint or glass being on someone's clothing by chance. Over three thousand paint fragments were found! Although most of them were very small, even extremely small paint samples can be analysed using modern techniques. If the paint is from a car, it is very often possible to deduce the make, model, and even the year it was built by comparing it with samples provided by the manufacturer.

The techniques used for examining small samples (i.e. emission spectroscopy, mass spectrometry, special methods of chromatography, etc. . . .) are beyond the scope of this book, but later in this chapter are described some activities which can be carried out on larger samples.

Also in the survey, glass fragments of many different types were found on the clothing. These fragments came from a variety of sources – broken bottles, light bulbs, windows, etc. Even for small pieces of the commonest types of window glass, the odds against having this glass on the clothing by chance were about 3000-1. So if a suspect has a fragment of glass on him which is exactly the same type as that from the scene of a crime, he will have some explaining to do! However, for a total identity to be made, the forensic scientist may well need a larger sample than he has available!

49

LOOKING MORE CLOSELY AT PAINT

The modern techniques generally used for examining paint in the forensic laboratory are too advanced to discuss here, but there are certain basic tests which are still often used, i.e.

- Observation under the microscope.
- Solubility in a selection of solvents.
- Chromatography techniques.

Paint samples generally appear either as chips or as smears. Paints which harden by evaporation of a solvent (e.g. cellulose car paint) tend to harden quite quickly and, when damaged, produce paint chips. However, there are some occasions when this is not necessarily true, for example, a glancing blow in a hit-and-run accident may only leave a smear of paint on the unfortunate victim.

Paints which harden by chemical reaction, e.g. oxidation, as in the case of many gloss paints used for woodwork, etc., generally take a long time to harden, and are often transferred as smears. Old gloss paint which has hardened will, of course, chip off and it is often possible to identify the different layers of paint which make up the chip. Recently, while carrying out some rebuilding work, the author found some paint chips with 21 clearly visible layers, while removing an old window frame. Under the low power microscope, it looked like the diagram below.

A paint chip viewed through a microscope

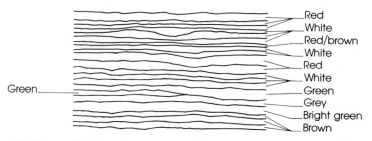

The likelihood of anyone walking around with paint chips like this on their clothing by sheer chance would be very remote indeed!

ACTIVITY 21

Looking at paint

Collect some paint chips from an old door or window, or from an old and frequently repainted car. Place the chip on a wooden bench mat and, holding it in place with a pair of tweezers, carefully cut a straight edge with a scalpel or sharp knife. Using the tweezers, pick up the paint chip and gently embed it into a piece of Plasticine or Blu-tack, placed on a microscope slide, with the freshly cut straight edge facing upwards.

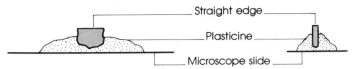

Straight edge

Plasticine

Microscope slide

Examining paint chips

Examine the edge of the paint chip under the low-power microscope and carefully make a note of what you see:

- How many layers of paint can you see?
- Are all the layers the same thickness?
- Are some layers uneven?
- What colours are present?
- What order are the colours found in?

Provided that the paint chip you selected had several layers, the chances of an identical chip being found elsewhere are quite remote. Evidence of this type can be quite damning on its own in court, but to back up such findings further tests can be carried out. Remember, you are normally trying to *compare* samples of paint – one sample from the scene of the crime, the other from the suspect.

ACTIVITY 22

Comparing paint samples

You are given two samples of paint chips which are similar in appearance. Alternatively, each person in the class could bring in some samples for *other* people to use. The two samples may both be from the same place or they may have been taken from completely different sources. That will be for you to find out!

Label one sample 'Paint from scene of crime', and the other sample 'Paint from suspect'. By carrying out the following tests you are trying to check whether the samples are from the same source, i.e. has the suspect been at the scene of the crime? Note, we cannot say at this stage whether the suspect actually committed the crime, only whether he was at the scene or not! It is not essential to carry out all of the tests – very often 1) and 2) alone will deny or confirm any similarities between the samples.

1) *Appearance*
   Examine the samples under the microscope as described in the previous activity.

2) *Testing the solubility of the paint samples*

Propanone (acetone)
Ethanol

Care!

Flammable!   *Harmful!*

51

Put some of each sample on to a spotting tile or microscope slide – only a small amount is needed. Add a few drops of propanone (acetone) to each sample.

Care! Most of the solvents that are suitable for this work are harmful/dangerous in some way. **Check with your teacher.**

Can you see your paint samples dissolving (or perhaps just some layers?). Does the paint begin to *bleed*, i.e. does the propanone (acetone) extract the colour from the paint without actually dissolving it?

Is there any noticeable change at all? Repeat, using fresh paint samples, with ethanol as a solvent. Again, carefully look for any changes. Ask your teacher what other solvents are available, and try those. Put your results into a table.

Solvent added to paint	Effect on paint from scene	Effect on paint from suspect
Propanone (acetone) Ethanol etc.		

3)   *Examining the colours of the paint*

Propanone
Ethanol
Ethyl ethanoate
Butanol
Ethanoic acid (acetic acid)

Flammable!   *Harmful!*   *Toxic!*

If any of the paint samples did bleed into the solvent, you may well be left with a coloured solution. It is often possible to examine these coloured solutions in more detail, in the same way that inks are investigated in Chapter 10 on Forgery i.e. using paper chromatography (Activity 24, p. 80). The only difference in procedure is that *water* is unlikely to separate out any individual dyes in your coloured solution, and you will almost certainly have to use some other solvent, or mixture of solvents. Which solvent to use is very often a matter of trial and error, but the following have been successful on many occasions:

- Propanone (acetone).

- Ethanol.

- Ethyl acetate (ethyl ethanoate) and acetic acid (ethanoic acid) in the ratio of 60:40 by volume.

- Butanol and water in the ratio of 50:50 by volume.

- Butanol, ethanol and ethanoic acid in the ratios of 60:20:20 by volume.

Try investigating your coloured solution using paper chromatography with one of the solvents/solvent mixtures suggested.

Remember: *Many of the solvents used are harmful. Use small quantities wherever possible. Make sure you know what the dangers are before you start.*

On occasions, a far simpler technique for comparison of paint chips may be employed. Consider the following case.

After a hit-and-run accident, several paint chips were found at the scene of the crime.

Paint chips found at the scene of the crime

After some investigation, the police tracked down a suspect vehicle whose nearside wing was damaged. Some paint chips from the damaged area were removed and taken for forensic examination. With larger paint chips, it is often possible to fit them together like a jig-saw. A perfect mechanical fit can provide conclusive evidence that the paint chips originated from the same place.

How the paint chips fit together

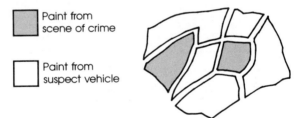

Paint from scene of crime

Paint from suspect vehicle

The same is true, of course, for glass fragments, particularly for headlamp, sidelight, or indicator glass on a vehicle where a patterned finish on the glass can assist the piecing together.

LOOKING MORE CLOSELY AT GLASS

Although there are many different types of glass, probably 99 per cent of the glass that the forensic scientist is asked to examine is from broken windows and car headlamps, etc. Chemically they are very similar indeed, and the scientist has to rely mainly on comparison of their *physical properties*.

If a glass fragment shows faces of the sheet that it came from, as in the following diagram then thickness can be measured and compared, but generally the fragments being looked at are too small. Some glass samples fluoresce under UV light, and this test can be used as a first check. If glass from a suspect vehicle's broken headlamp fluoresces, but glass from the scene of the hit-and-run doesn't, there would be little point in investigating further.

A glass fragment

The two most useful techniques for comparing glass samples are:

- Density (though little used nowadays in routine forensic work).

- Refractive index measurements.

Both of these properties can vary considerably amongst common glass types, yet can be measured very accurately using small fragments.

Density

This is a measure of how closely packed together the particles are in a material (i.e. mass per unit volume). The densities of glasses may vary due to differences in the amounts of various chemicals that they contain, e.g. more lead – denser glass. Density can be measured by a method called *flotation*.

If a liquid or mixture of liquids can be found in which glass fragments neither sink nor float, their densities are indentical with that of the liquid (NB   Density varies with temperature – so the temperature during the test has to be kept constant.) It is not necessary to actually measure the density, it is sufficient to show that glass from the scene and glass from the suspect remain stationary in the same liquid, at the same temperature, i.e. the glass samples have the same density.

Refractive index

This is a measure of the amount light bends, or *refracts*, when it passes through a substance.

Bending of light through glass

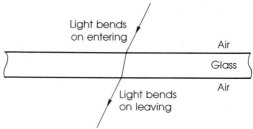

All glass samples will bend light in this way, but very often by substantially different amounts.

If a colourless piece of glass is put into a colourless liquid such as water, you can still see the glass fragment. This is because the glass and the water have *different* refractive indices. However, the refractive index of a solid such as glass hardly changes at all if the temperature is varied, but those of liquids change considerably. Therefore, if we heat up a liquid, at some stage the refractive index of the liquid will equal the glass and the glass will seem to disappear. If glass from the scene of the crime and glass from a suspect disappear at the same time (i.e. at the same temperature) then they have identical refractive indices. If this is so, then the glass samples could have come from the same source or from different panes of glass with the same properties. Whichever is true will depend on how common or rare the refractive index value is. The forensic scientist can refer to 'frequency of occurrence' charts which give him some idea of how much weight he can give to his evidence.

The refractive index of glasses

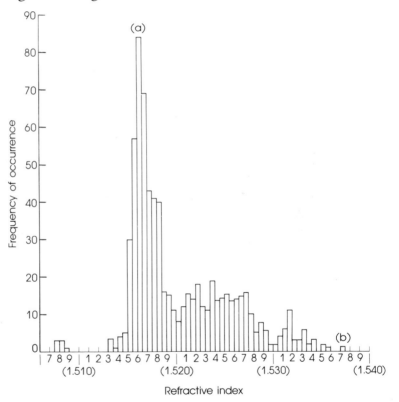

A more commonly occurring glass such as (a) would have less value as evidence than, say, glass (b) which is quite rarely found. To find glass (b) on a suspect's clothing by sheer chance would be much more unlikely.

The forensic scientist is nowadays beginning to face problems, however, in his investigation of glass. More and more of our glass is being manufactured by larger, but fewer, companies.

With more automation and carefully controlled processes, the glass being produced shows a lot less variation than in the past. Therefore, as old glass is replaced by standardised modern glass, it is becoming much more difficult to distinguish samples. Glass used in bottles, headlamps, etc., still uses a lot of recycled glass and its properties will still vary considerably, but comparison of window glass is difficult because of this standardisation.

QUESTIONS ON CHAPTER 7

1 A pedestrian was knocked over by a car. The driver failed to stop after the accident, and there were no witnesses. The only lead the police had was the discovery of some paint chippings and some broken headlamp glass at the scene of the crime. Below are diagrams showing the shapes of the pieces of glass found at the scene and also some pieces of glass removed from the headlamp of a suspect's car.

(a) Is there any obvious match between the glass samples from these two sources? Which piece(s), if any, of glass from the scene fit the headlamp glass from the suspect vehicle?

Fragments of glass

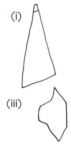
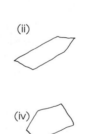

(b) The paint from the scene was also compared with paint samples from the suspect vehicle. Below are diagrams of the samples showing the paint layers in each. Choose one paint fragment from each sample that you think match up.

Fragments of paint

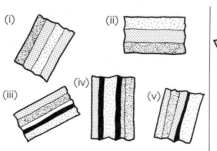
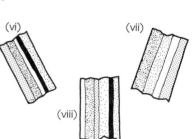

(c) If the suspect car is the one that was involved in the accident, why don't all of the paint samples match up? Give reasons.

2 Given two paint chips – one from the scene of a burglary and the other from a suspect's clothing – outline briefly what tests you would carry out in order to compare the samples.

3 Why is the comparison of window glass samples becoming increasingly difficult, yet the comparison of glass samples from bottles or headlamps is still largely successful?

WORDFINDER FOR PAINT AND GLASS

Look carefully at the following questions and statements, and write down your answers to each one. If your answers are correct, you should be able to find them in the word square below.

1 Paint is normally transferred either as smears or
    _____ (6)
2 Hardening of paints by chemical reaction (9)
3 Some paints harden by evaporation of a _____ (7)
4 A possible solvent for some paints (9)
5 Extracting the colour from paint without actually dissolving it (8)
6 Generally, glass samples are compared by looking at their _____ properties (8)
7 Density can be measured by a method called _____ (9)
8 _____ _____ is a measure of the amount light bends when it passes through a substance such as glass (10, 5)
9 This type of crime may involve broken glass (8)

A E R O X Y A R E L N O I T A T O L F I
A L E B L C R O H P Q X A R E F E A O P
X T V O A S G A R C R S E K A L F U G E
H N I F C D A I L F G O R B A C Y R D C
I E T K I J I E H G S N P N O S T A W E
S V C F S Y N C A T R D I A R E A S E D
O L A D Y E D H A U B U R D N I B E Y C
C O R L H G E J B Y D F B H E O F H A L
Z S F G P O X I D A T I O N U E N M V G
G K E A D K C O L R E H S T E H L E C A
E V R I B W Y A Q S E M L O H U J B O X

CHAPTER 8
THE WORK OF THE FORENSIC BIOLOGIST

The work of the forensic biologist covers a vast area. He or she could be asked to identify bloodstains and their blood groups, identify stains of other body fluids, e.g. sweat, urine, saliva, etc., identify samples of animal and plant tissue, compare and identify hairs, fibres and fabrics, etc.

Perhaps the two most familiar areas of his or her work are the examination of blood samples/stains following a violent crime and the examination of fibres and fabrics.

LOOKING AT BLOOD

Whenever blood is associated with a crime, the identification of *whose* blood it is becomes vitally important. It may arise from a violent crime, a burglar cutting himself or, for that matter, an injury to an animal (e.g. as in sheep worrying). The first priority is to confirm that the stain is, in fact, blood, and then to determine whether it is human or animal blood.

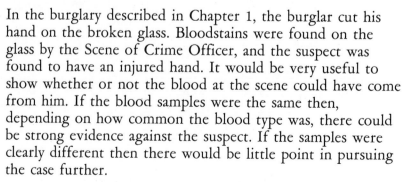

In the burglary described in Chapter 1, the burglar cut his hand on the broken glass. Bloodstains were found on the glass by the Scene of Crime Officer, and the suspect was found to have an injured hand. It would be very useful to show whether or not the blood at the scene could have come from him. If the blood samples were the same then, depending on how common the blood type was, there could be strong evidence against the suspect. If the samples were clearly different then there would be little point in pursuing the case further.

Blood is made up of *red blood cells*, *white blood cells*, and *platelets* floating around in a watery liquid called *plasma*. The red blood cells may contain substances called *A* and *B*. The plasma may also contain substances called *antibodies*.

When a sample of human blood is examined under a microscope, it has the following appearance.

58

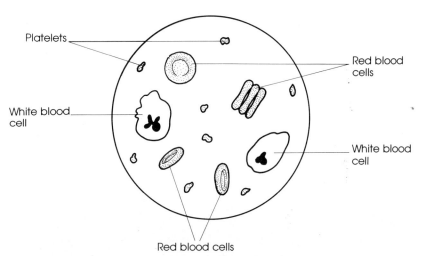

Highly magnified blood sample

Platelets

White blood cell

Red blood cells

Red blood cells

White blood cell

However, forensic comparison of blood does *not* involve microscopic examination. Instead, it often relies upon the interaction of substances A and/or B with antibodies. When an antibody from one type of blood meets red blood cells from another type of blood, it can cause the red blood cells to clump together:

- The antibody called *anti-A* causes clumping of red blood cells containing A.

- The antibody called *anti-B* causes clumping of red blood cells containing B.

By mixing blood samples with anti-A and anti-B we can see when clumping occurs, and we can therefore identify whether a person has substance A or substance B, or both, or neither in his red blood cells.

Blood group	Red blood cells contain substance	Antibody present in plasma
A	A	anti-B
B	B	anti-A
AB	A and B	neither
O	neither	anti-A and anti-B

This is called the *ABO system* of blood grouping. Group O is the most common (47 per cent of the population are group O) and group AB is the least common (3 per cent of the population are group AB).

In the past many schools have carried out practical work on blood grouping, using blood grouping cards.

The card carries anti-A and anti-B impregnated on to it (i.e. in boxes (a) and (b) of the following diagram). When red blood cells from a group A person are mixed with anti-A clumping occurs, but not when mixed with Anti-B. Cells from group O are not affected by either antibody, but those from group AB would be clumped in both. The 'control' contains neither antibody and should not clump with any blood sample.

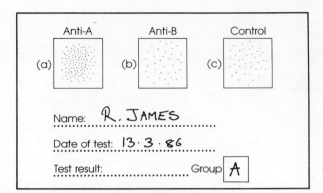

A blood grouping card

Such practical tests are nowadays discouraged, being seen as unnecessary risks of infection, but details are given in many biology text books.

In addition to the ABO blood grouping system, there are over a dozen other ways of classifying blood samples. If blood from a suspect differs from blood from the scene in any one of these systems, then the suspect cannot possibly be guilty! If the blood samples show the same *combination* of groups, then it is possible that he may be guilty. The most common combination of groups would represent about 0.25 per cent of the population (i.e. about 1 person in every 600). The rare combination of groups could almost isolate one person out of the entire world's population!

FIBRES AND FABRICS

Although hairs (human or animal) and fibres very often look quite similar to the naked eye, they are clearly different when viewed under the microscope (see Activity 1, p. 9). Comparison of individual fibres, and the fabrics that they come from, is not always quite so straightforward, however. The forensic scientist might be faced with examining minute fibres rubbed off a criminal's clothes, or, with luck, a larger piece of fabric which has caught on some sharp object as the criminal committed the crime.

Fibres can either be *natural*, i.e. obtained from plants (e.g. cotton) and animals (e.g. wool), or *man-made* (*synthetic*) (e.g. nylon, terylene, etc.).

As a general guide, a natural fibre tends to have a rough and irregular appearance, whereas man-made fibres are longer and smoother, although some manufacturing processes can change the appearance quite dramatically.

Microscope
Micrometer
Strength.

Fibres

(a) Wool fibre: rough, scaly appearance

(b) Cotton fibre: twisted fibres easily grip each other

(c) Nylon: longer, smoother and straighter than (a) and (b)

If the forensic scientist is fortunate enough to receive a larger piece of fabric to examine, then in addition to looking at the fibres themselves, he or she can also investigate how the fibres are woven into the fabric.

Individual fibres of a material are made into yarn which is then either woven or knitted to make a fabric. There are many ways in which the yarn may be woven or knitted.

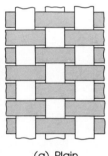

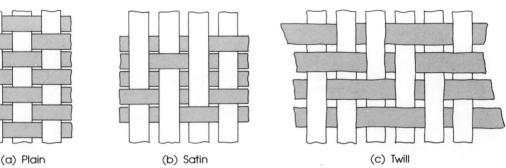

(a) Plain

(b) Satin

(c) Twill

Fabrics

The distinctive patterns can be identified using a hand lens or low power microscope. Go back to Activity 1 and carefully examine a variety of fabrics. Try to identify the pattern of weaving used.

The forensic scientist may well use a special sort of microscope when trying to compare fibres from the scene of a crime with fibres from a suspect's clothing – the *comparison microscope*. This consists of two separate microscopes linked by an 'optical bridge' which allows the user to view two objects side by side, using only one eyepiece.

If the fibres appear to be the same, then it could well be that they came from the same place. The temptation to say that the suspect must have been at the scene of the crime still has to be resisted, however. As with the investigation of glass, it depends on how common the particular fibres are. If the fibres came from a jumper which could be bought in shops up and down the country, then very little weight could be placed on this evidence. However, if several different fibres from the scene matched up with the suspect's clothes (e.g.

61

fibres from his jumper, jacket, trousers, etc.) then the odds of finding some other suspect with a similar *combination* of clothes are much more remote and the police would have a much stronger case to go to court with!

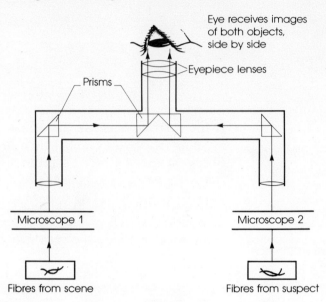

Eye receives images of both objects, side by side

Eyepiece lenses

Prisms

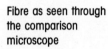

The comparison microscope

Microscope 1

Microscope 2

Fibres from scene

Fibres from suspect

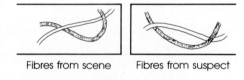

Fibre as seen through the comparison microscope

Fibres from scene

Fibres from suspect

QUESTIONS ON CHAPTER 8

THINKS

1 (a) Explain simply what is meant by the *ABO system* of blood grouping.

(b) When might the police need to compare blood groupings?

(c) If a murder victim had blood group AB, and blood of this group was also found on a suspect's clothing, would this provide strong evidence that the suspect was the murderer? Explain your answer.

(d) If the blood group in (c) was group O instead of group AB, would this make any difference to the strength of the evidence?

2 (a) Explain briefly how you could tell the difference between a man-made fibre such as nylon, and a natural fibre such as wool.

(b) A wool fibre found at the scene of a crime matched fibres from a suspect's pullover. What additional information would be needed before the forensic biologist could give an opinion about the strength of the evidence?

3 Logic problem

Following a burglary, the SOCO found three fibres at the scene which were then sent to the forensic biologist for examination. From the clues given below, see if you can work out what colour each fibre was, what article of clothing it came from, and in which room of the burgled house it was found. Copy and complete the chart, writing √ for a definite 'yes' and X for a definite 'no'. Information from the first two clues has already been entered on the chart for you.

	Red	Black	Green	Wool	Nylon	Cotton	Jacket	Coat	Scarf
Bedroom	√	✗	✗						
Kitchen	✗								
Lounge	✗	✗						✗	
Jacket						√			
Coat						✗			
Scarf						✗			
Wool					✗				
Nylon	✗	✗	√						
Cotton					✗				

Clues

(a) The red fibre was found in the bedroom.
(b) The green article of clothing was made of nylon.
(c) The cotton fibre was found to have come from the jacket.
(d) The fibre from the black coat was not found in the lounge.

THE WORK OF THE FORENSIC TOXICOLOGIST

Toxicology is the study of substances which are harmful to human beings. The work of the forensic toxicologist generally falls into three main areas (although this may vary from laboratory to laboratory):

- Routine testing for alcohol in blood/urine samples following a 'breathalyser' test. However, with the introduction of new procedures, much of the 'alcohol testing' of motorists is carried out solely by the police with fewer cases being passed on to the forensic laboratory.

- Identification of drugs such as heroin, cannabis, etc., the possession and use of which is controlled by law.

- Analysis of organs, tissues and body fluids in cases of suspected poisoning (accidental and deliberate).

The most publicised area of work in recent years, even though it is not the most important, has been the routine testing for alcohol, and this is described first.

MEASURING ALCOHOL IN THE BLOOD

When someone drinks something alcoholic, the alcohol is eventually absorbed into the bloodstream. It is then taken to all parts of the body, including the brain, where it has an effect on the nervous system. This makes any motorist potentially unsafe. The more alcohol that is drunk, the higher the proportion of alcohol in the blood. In the UK the law says that no one should be driving a vehicle if they have more than 80 mg of alcohol per 100 cm^3 of blood. The penalties for breaking this law can be severe – disqualification from driving, payment of a fine, or even a prison sentence.

Alcohol is a drug which affects the nervous system. Even small amounts in the bloodstream, less than the legal limit for drivers, can reduce judgement and driving skills. About one third of all road accidents are connected with alcohol. In the year that the breathalyser was introduced in the UK, there were 40 000 fewer accidents on the roads and over 1100 fewer deaths.

The method used to check whether a motorist is over the legal limit has changed in recent years. Up until a few years ago, a roadside breath test was first carried out. If this proved positive then further tests were carried out at the forensic laboratories on a blood or urine sample from the driver, to determine the accurate level of alcohol present. Nowadays, an electronic roadside *breath-screening* device (the *Lion Alcolmeter*) is used. It is accurate, reliable and simple to use. On its own, however, it is insufficient to present to court as evidence.

The law in this country insists that a driver who 'fails' this first test should then be taken to a police station and asked to undergo a further test on a substantive breath-testing machine (the *Intoximeter*) which has been approved by the Secretary of State. The results from this *can* be used as evidence in court, and the forensic scientist may have no involvement in the case at all. It is only when the concentration of alcohol in the breath, as shown by the Intoximeter, falls within a certain range that the driver may request the analysis of a blood or urine sample at the forensic science laboratory.

Descriptions of both systems are given in this chapter, i.e:

- The 'old' procedure – the breath test, followed by blood/urine tests.

- The 'new' procedure – the Lion Alcolmeter, followed by the Intoximeter, with further possible tests on blood or urine samples at the forensic laboratory.

Comparing the two illustrates very clearly the rapid advances of technology in the last few years. Only by using the very latest technology can the police, and the forensic scientist, hope to keep up with and combat the increasing rate of crime.

The 'tube and bag' type of breathalyser

This type of breathalyser was not an accurate test, but it did give the police a rough idea of a person's state, and they could then decide whether it was worthwhile pursuing the matter further. If there was alcohol in a person's blood, there would also be alcohol in that person's *exhaled* or *breathed out* air. The more alcohol in the blood, the higher the concentration of alcohol in the air exhaled. The suspect driver was asked to blow through a tube into a plastic bag. The tube contained orange/yellow crystals of a chemical called potassium dichromate(VII). When this chemical comes into contact with alcohol, it reacts and its colour changes to green. The more alcohol there is present, the more crystals change colour. Marked on the tube was a line placed at the point where, if there were 80 milligrams of alcohol per 100 cm^3 of blood, the crystals on one side would remain yellow and those on the other side would change to green. If the crystals turned to green on *both* sides of the line, then it could well have been that the driver was over the legal limit.

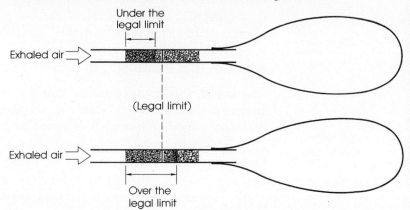

The breathalyser

The possible penalties for drunken driving can be quite severe and, in fairness to the driver, he or she was then asked to cooperate with a more accurate test which was carried out in the laboratory. The driver was asked by the police to provide either a blood or urine sample, which was then sent to the forensic laboratory for analysis. Failure to provide a sample was also an offence and carried equally harsh penalties.

At the forensic laboratory, the samples were tested by a machine which used a method called *gas chromatography*. This technique is similar in some ways to the paper chromatography method, that you may use to separate the different dyes in ink samples, except that a flow of gas passes through a tube rather than a solvent passing up the filter paper. (See Chapter 10 for further details of paper chromatography.) Calculating the amount of alcohol in the blood sample was a complex procedure, normally carried out by a computer linked to the machine. This produced greater accuracy, and saved an enormous amount of time for the forensic scientist in what was (and still is) considered to be a particularly tedious and routine job.

The accurate part of the procedure, therefore, was carried out at the forensic laboratory by determining *directly* how much alcohol was in a blood sample. With modern procedures, i.e. the use of the Alcolmeter and Intoximeter, direct examination of the blood is not necessary. Both of the modern devices rely on measurement of *breath alcohol concentration*.

Once alcohol is absorbed into the bloodstream, it is distributed around the rest of the body tissues. In the lungs, oxygen from the air passes into the blood, exchanging places with the waste products e.g. carbon dioxide. In the same way that carbon dioxide passes from the blood into the lungs, so too does a small representative portion of the alcohol.

How the breathalyser works

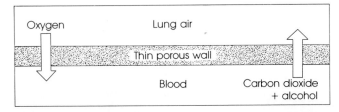

The amount of alcohol that evaporates into the breath depends on its concentration in the blood. This is known as *Henry's Law*, and it means that the breath alcohol level depends on the blood alcohol concentration. By measuring the level of alcohol in the breath we can, therefore, calculate the concentration of alcohol in the blood. So, how exactly do the modern breath-testing devices work?

The electronic device: The Lion Alcolmeter S-L2

The Lion Alcolmeter S-L2 uses a *fuel cell*, containing two platinum electrodes, to detect and measure the concentration of alcohol vapour in expired breath. A fuel cell is a device which can convert the chemical energy in a fuel, together with oxygen, directly into electrical energy.

| *hydrogen* (from alcohol) | + | *oxygen* (from the air) | → | *water* | + | *electrical energy* |

The fuel cell in the Lion Alcolmeter uses the alcohol in the expired breath as its source of fuel. When breath is passed into the fuel cell, a small voltage is produced if alcohol is present. The greater the amount of alcohol in the breath, the greater the voltage produced. This voltage is fed to an *electronic amplifier* and displayed on a series of three *alcohol level display lights* to show whether the driver's blood alcohol concentration is above or below the legal limit. Two additional *breath-sampling lights* tell the police officer whether the driver is blowing hard enough, and when enough breath has been blown into the device for it to make an accurate examination of the sample. The entire procedure only takes about one minute to complete, and the device is accurate, reliable, and simple to use. The results from the test are also decisive from the police officer's point of view. If the 'pass' light comes on, that is the end of the matter. If 'pass' and 'fail' both light up, the driver will receive a warning. However, if the 'fail' light alone illuminates, then a further breath test will be required at the police station using the larger Intoximeter machine, described later in this chapter.

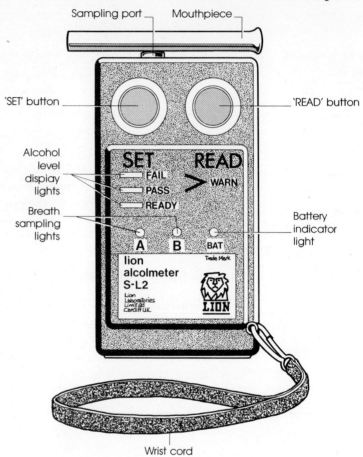

Sampling port — Mouthpiece —

'SET' button

'READ' button

Alcohol level display lights

Breath sampling lights

The Lion Alcolmeter S-L2

Battery indicator light

SET READ
FAIL
PASS > WARN
READY
A B BAT

lion
alcolmeter
S-L2
Lion
Laboratories
Limited
Cardiff U.K.
Trade Mark
LION

Wrist cord

The SET button This forms part of the sampling system. When the button is pressed, it locks to set the instrument ready for sampling. When the button rises, the sample to be analysed is drawn into the fuel cell detector.
The READ button This serves two purposes:

- To release the SET button, so that a sample is then taken.

- To switch on the amplifier and display lights.

Battery indicator light When lit, it shows that the battery has sufficient power for the Alcolmeter to operate.
Breath sampling lights Light 'A' shows that the subject is blowing hard enough. Light 'B' lights up when the subject has provided enough of a breath sample for the Alcolmeter to produce a reading.

Using the Lion
Alcolmeter S-L2

Alcohol level display lights Three lights, coloured green, amber, and red (marked READY, PASS, and FAIL), light up to show the range in which the blood alcohol concentration of the driver lies.

Sampling port This forms the entrance to the fuel cell detector.

Mouthpiece This is attached to the sampling port. For reasons of hygiene, a new mouthpiece is used for each individual test.

The Intoximeter

The Intoximeter can produce a fast, accurate tamper-proof measurement of a driver's breath-alcohol concentration. As the results of the test can be used as evidence in court, it means that the routine involvement of a doctor (to collect blood samples) and the forensic scientist (to analyse the blood sample) is no longer needed.

Although the design of the machine, and the accompanying electronics, represent the most up-to-date technology available, the basic principle of the alcohol measuring device, i.e. infrared analysis, is well known. In simple terms, when infrared light is shone through certain chemicals, it is absorbed. If infrared light of different wavelengths is used, some wavelengths are absorbed more than others. The result is a *spectrum* for that particular chemical. With ethanol (the alcohol in alcoholic drinks), we get a display as shown below.

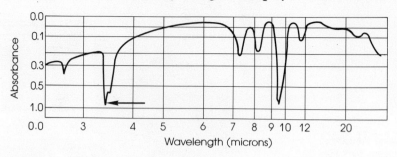

Spectrum produced by the Intoximeter

For infrared light of wavelength 6 microns, virtually none of the light is absorbed. However, for other wavelengths, e.g. 3.4 or 9.5 microns, there is much more light absorbed. (There are more up-to-date units for wavelength, but microns are still largely the actual unit used.)

Ethanol will always produce a spectrum of this basic pattern. The spectrum can be thought of as the 'fingerprint' for ethanol. Although the peaks are always in the same place, i.e. always at the same wavelengths, their size depends on how much light is actually absorbed by the ethanol being analysed. This depends on how much alcohol is in the sample. The bigger the peak, the more alcohol present, and, therefore, by measuring the peak we can calculate the concentration of ethanol in the breath sample.

The Intoximeter in use

The Intoximeter is made up of three main parts:

- The infrared analyser section.

- The computer section.

- The breath simulator.

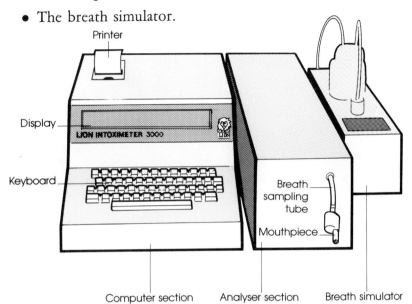

Printer

Display

LION INTOXIMETER 3000

Keyboard

Breath sampling tube

Mouthpiece

Computer section   Analyser section   Breath simulator

In the *infrared analyser* section (see diagram below) the infrared source sends infrared light through a double-chambered container, to an infrared detector. One of the chambers (the bottom one in the diagram) is the sample chamber into which the breath sample (70 ml) has been blown. The other chamber is the 'reference chamber' containing no alcohol. The infrared detector compares the infrared light from the sample chamber with that from the reference chamber, and determines the amount of alcohol present in the sample. This information could be presented as a spectrum produced by a chart recorder. The peaks could then be measured and the concentration of the alcohol calculated.

The infrared analyser section of the Intoximeter

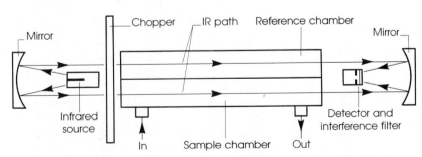

Mirror   Chopper   IR path   Reference chamber   Mirror

Infrared source   In   Sample chamber   Out   Detector and interference filter

In the Intoximeter, however, the information is passed directly from the IR detector to the *computer* where it is processed electronically and displayed on a display panel. All of the readings/results of the test are also printed out on paper as a permanent record. The keyboard allows the operator to type in details of the motorist, i.e. name, address, date of birth, etc., but it cannot be used to alter the clock or date, nor can it be used to make any changes to the 'alcohol readings' produced by the machine.

The third section of the machine – the *breath simulator* – automatically checks that accurate results are being given. It injects an air/alcohol vapour mixture of known concentration into the instrument which is then analysed. If the concentration of alcohol detected by the machine is the same as that concentration fed into it, then obviously accurate results are being given. Calibration checks such as this are carried out before and after the motorist has given breath samples, to ensure that any fault which may occur with the machine is identified at once – a useful safeguard from the motorist's point of view.

IDENTIFICATION OF DRUGS

The toxicologist is often asked to identify a substance which is found in a person's possession and which is thought to be a drug controlled by law. Many of these substances are habit-forming drugs which lead to addiction and death, and so the law in this country forbids their possession (except under very restricted circumstances, e.g. when prescribed by a doctor, etc.).

The Misuse of Drugs Act (1971) governs the manufacture and supply of controlled drugs for genuine medical use. However, the Act makes it a criminal offence unlawfully to manufacture, supply or possess a controlled drug. A drug controlled under the Act is placed in one of three classes. The most dangerous drugs, e.g. heroin, opium, etc., fall into class A and offences involving these drugs are severely punished. Class B drugs such as cannabis carry less punishment, and class C carry the lowest penalties. Some of the more commonly found, and misused, drugs are shown in the table below, and grouped as classified by the 1971 Act.

Class A	Class B	Class C
heroin	amphetamine	benzphetamine
morphine	cannabis	diethylpropion
opium	codeine	chlorphentermine
LSD	dihydrocodeine	
pethidine		pipradrol
cocaine		

When offences involving these drugs are brought to the courts, it is necessary to prove that a substance found in someone's possession really *is* a drug covered by the Act. It falls to the toxicologist to carry out this identification.

There are many ways that he can go about tackling the problem of identification. Many drugs are available as commercially prepared capsules or tablets, and some may be recognised by colour, size, shape or markings. However, the substance would still need to be analysed to *confirm* its identity. The toxicologist depends largely on various types of chromatography in order to carry out this identification, e.g. paper chromatography (as discussed in Chapter 10 on Forgeries), thin-layer chromatography, gas-liquid chromatography (as used in blood/alcohol measurements), and more recently, high pressure liquid chromatography. Such techniques can detect tiny traces of drugs, and concentrations of a drug as low as 10^{-9} g in 20 cm^3 of solvent can be measured.

Although being superseded on many occasions by high pressure liquid chromatography, thin-layer chromatography still has an important place in the range of tools available to the forensic scientist.

Thin-layer chromatography is similar in many respects to paper chromatography. Instead of using paper, however, a glass plate covered with a thin layer of an absorbent material such as alumina is used. A small drop of the substance to be tested is placed on the the alumina on the plate near one end, and allowed to soak in and dry.

Thin-layer chromatography

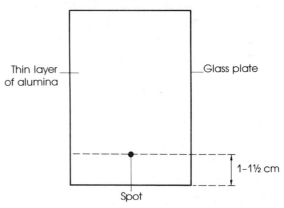

The plate is then lowered into a solvent with the spot just above the liquid level. As the solvent rises up the plate, so the substance(s) in the spot do as well. Different substances move up the plate at different rates, and if the spot contained a mixture of substances, then they will be separated and appear at different heights. When the solvent front has almost reached the top of the plate, the plate is removed from the solvent, allowed to dry and then sprayed with a chemical that reacts with the drugs being tested for. By examining what colours are produced, the toxicologist can determine what class of compounds the substance in the spot belongs to. In addition, by looking at the height the spot travelled up the plate compared with the height reached by the solvent, he can identify the actual drug involved.

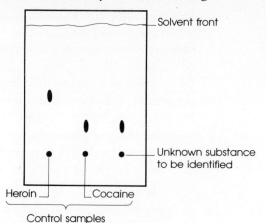

Testing for cocaine

In the diagram, the spot of the unknown substance found on a suspect matches a control sample of cocaine in both colour and position. The unknown substance is therefore, cocaine.

In addition to these chromatography techniques, however, such methods as X-ray diffraction and infrared and ultraviolet spectrophotometry are also widely used for the analysis and identification of suspected drugs. In recent times, increasing general use has been made in many toxicology departments of a method involving both gas-liquid chromatography and mass spectrometry. This combined method has proved to be a powerful tool for working out the structure of many substances, leading on to their identification. Mass spectrometry is discussed further in the next section.

ANALYSIS OF ORGANS, TISSUES AND BODY FLUIDS

The third main area of toxicology work involves the analysis of organs, tissues, and body fluids in cases of sudden death, suspected poisonings, etc. The number of deaths in the UK each year as a result of poisoning (either accidental or deliberate) runs into many thousands. A post-mortem examination is carried out after each such death by a pathologist, who sends specimens of various body tissues, etc., to the toxicologist in the laboratory. In suspected poisonings, the stomach and its contents, the liver, intestines, blood and urine samples may all be sent to the toxicologist for examination, in an attempt to identify the poison.

This area of work also involves the use of chromatography methods to identify possible poisons found in the body. In addition, however, scanning electron microscopes, emission spectrographs and atomic absorption instruments are used to detect heavy metals such as thallium, mercury, and lead, which are frequently found in poisoning cases. Of particular importance, though, is the mass spectrometer which is capable of investigating very small samples. A detailed explanation of how the mass spectrometer works is beyond the scope of this book, but a simplified account is given below.

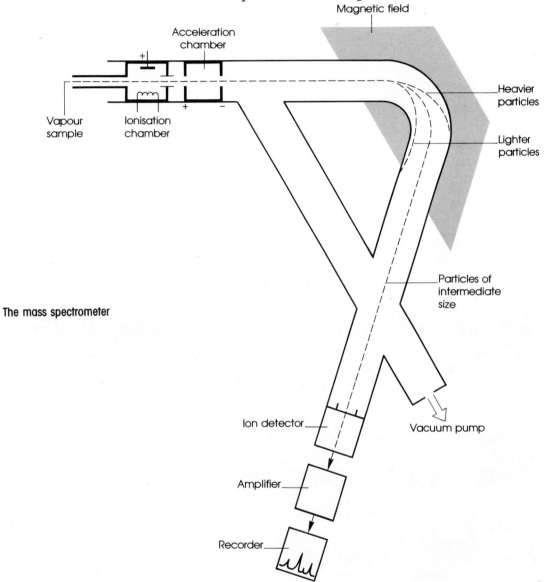

The mass spectrometer

There are five main stages in the mass spectrometer.
1) The sample which is to be tested is turned into a *vapour* by heating.
2) The vapour is bombarded by electrons; this gives the vapour particles an electrical charge (positive). These charged particles are called *ions*.

3) The positive ions are required to move through the apparatus very quickly, and so at this stage they are *accelerated* (by an electric field).

4) The fast moving positive ions move between strong magnets which *deflect* them. Light particles are deflected more than heavier ones.

5) As the deflected ions pass out of the magnetic field they are *detected* by an ion detector, and their presence and number recorded as a graph.

If the strength of the magnetic field is changed, the lighter and heavier particles shown on the diagram can also be made to hit the detector. There is a mathematical link between the *strength of the magnetic field* needed to make the ions hit the detector, and the *mass* of the ions. We can, therefore, work out what the mass of the ion is. Once the mass of the ion (or *ions*) is known, the identity of the original substance can be worked out.

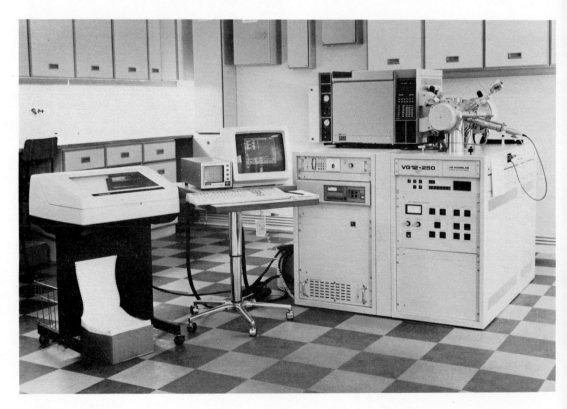

The VG Masslab gas chromatography/ quadrupole mass spectrometer

The instrument shown in the photograph is particularly well suited to forensic analysis. This gas chromatography/mass spectrometer system is capable of rapid screening of a wide variety of drugs and poisons. It is possible to identify the main drugs or poisons in samples even as small as 10^{-12} g.

THINKS

QUESTIONS ON CHAPTER 9

1 Here are some statistics for road accidents.

Road accidents in Newtown for the year 1984

A	Total accidents	...250
	Accidents resulting in death	... 25

B	Accidents to pedestrians	... 70
	Accidents to cyclists	 35
	Accidents to car drivers	... 20
	Accidents to car passengers	... 80
	Accidents to motor cyclists	... 45

C	Clothes worn by pedestrians in accidents:	
	Dark overcoats	... 58
	White or bright clothes	... 6
	Fluorescent arm bands	... 5
	White clothes and armbands	... 1

D	Age of pedestrians in accidents:	
	Over 60	... 25
	15 and over	... 15
	5 to 15	... 35
	under 5	... 5

(a) Copy the axes below on to graph paper and draw a bar graph to show the information in Section B.

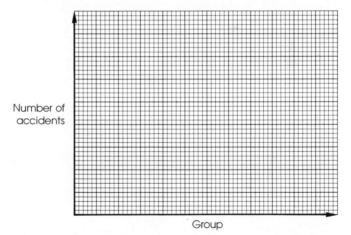

Bar graph showing number of accidents

Number of accidents

Group

(b) What fraction of the people in accidents died?

(c) What is this fraction expressed as a percentage?

(d) What information do the statistics give you about the sort of clothes you should wear if you are a pedestrian, to stand the best chance of not having an accident?

(e) What would be the best clothes to wear at night? Give a reason for your answer.

(f) In which age range do pedestrians have the most road accidents?

(g) Give a reason why under fives have fewer accidents than the 5 to 15s.

WORDFINDER FOR THE WORK OF THE FORENSIC TOXICOLOGIST

Unscramble the jumbled up names of the drugs listed below, then try to find each word in the word square. The answers may read across from left to right, or from right to left, or diagonally, or upwards or downwards. Copy the square on to a piece of paper and ring your answers. Do not write on this page. The first one is done for you!

1 HENORI   Heroin   2 ISBANCAN
3 NOIRMPHE   4 TEAMIPHAMEN
5 UMOPI   6 ENOCIDE
7 ECAINOC   8 THINPEDIE

```
A P Q B A F Q F P E D A C I M E H
V H E O S C S J O E P M I J G P I
B O T M R F U E D U M C M Y A T G
U V D V O G N S E B L O G Y W A Q
H R I J X I I C E L H V L T P O S
M O Y T O E L W U A P A U I W E I
D J M R Z B Y G T D L X U V N I B
Q T E X I A C L O Z U B U D O E A
S H E M C R I D X H S L C O F Z N
A M P H E T A M I N E S U A L U N
G P C U B T E N I H P R O M S E A
R A B J E D H I T G O I J U O U C
C Y C U X G E M C J B D Q E A E L
O P A X B P H U T A Z B Z N S F I
C S V Q D Y Q I J R T K R I X U X
A R C E G B H P O W C D V E Y R K
I U V D U P T O H X U B O D U W A
N S G Y K I S P U E N E Y O N I F
E V U B Q X F T H O V B U C O P N
R G V K O S K H W A X H W R E B I
S X G H E N I D I H T E P O U M R
```

FORGERY

The forging of documents, most commonly cheques, is normally carried out by forging a signature, erasing something and writing something else instead, or simply overwriting (as in the case of our burglar in Chapter 1). The examination of the handwriting of a suspected forged signature would be undertaken by a handwriting expert, but where changes are made to a document, the investigation may be undertaken by the forensic chemist.

Inks commonly found in writing can sometimes be removed by using a bleach which chemically changes the dyes in the ink from coloured to colourless (and hence invisible), without significantly damaging the paper. When writing is erased in this way, observation under UV light very often shows up fluorescence due to chemical bleaching or a dark outline where the writing has been removed. In this way, cheques that have been changed, or motor car tax discs that have been altered, etc., can often be readily identified. Similarly, observations under infrared radiation can also identify altered documents, and this is nowadays probably used more than ultraviolet light.

Erasing ink

Many ink pens are available nowadays which have a normal ink at one end and a liquid 'eraser' at the other. Write something down on paper and erase half of it. What does it look like under: (a) a low power microscope, (b) a UV lamp?

If you do not have one of these 'magic' pens, write something out in normal ink and carefully paint (using a fine brush) some ordinary household bleach over part of the writing. It should work just as well, i.e. remove your writing.

A great deal of forgery is carried out, however, simply by overwriting, for example, a cheque made out for seven pounds can easily be changed into one for seventy.

Generally, this type of forgery can be detected quite easily by showing that two different inks have been used, one ink for writing 'seven' and a second ink for writing 'ty'. There are three main ways in which the inks can be shown to be different: using *chromatography*; using *ultraviolet light*; using *infrared radiation*.

A forged cheque

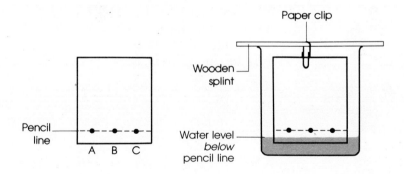

60-04-09

1st April 1986

Pay Cash

Seventy pounds — or order

£ 70

MR. J. SMITH

J Smith

ıı°0004 2 2ıı° 60ın04 09ı: 47 10 74 56ıı°

CHROMATOGRAPHY

Many inks are made up of mixtures of dyes. Chromatography is a method which separates the dyes in a mixture so that we can see what different colour dyes were used to make the ink. If you were given three samples of black ink which looked identical, you could well find that they all differ considerably when the mixtures in them are separated out.

ACTIVITY 24

Comparing inks using chromatography

Cut some strips of filter paper, as shown in the diagram. Draw a pencil line across the paper about 1 cm up from the bottom edge. On the pencil line, make some ink blobs using gelt or fibre tip pens (black or brown will probably give the best results).

Comparing inks

Paper clip

Wooden splint

Pencil line

A   B   C

Water level below pencil line

Suspend the filter paper in a beaker with some water as shown, and leave it until the water has soaked up through the filter paper, almost to the top. As water moves through the ink samples, up the filter paper, different dyes in the inks move up the filter paper with the water, *but at different rates.*

The resulting filter paper showing the separated dyes is called a *chromatogram.*

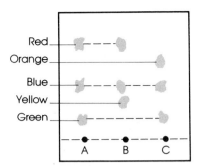

The chromatogram

Each of these three inks contain a different combination of dyes, for example:

- Ink A – green, blue, red.
- Ink B – yellow, blue, red.
- Ink C – green, blue, orange.

Also, even though they all contain some blue dye, it may well be that the intensity of the blue spots could vary considerably, perhaps with a faint blue spot from ink A, but a very intense blue spot from ink B and/or C.

NB   Some inks are not soluble in water, particularly ball-point pen inks, and a different solvent may have to be used instead of the water. Methanol is quite a good alternative, but trial and error is very often the only way to find out which solvent is the most suitable.

Samples of ink from a forged cheque could be treated in this way to establish whether they were different.

USING ULTRAVIOLET LIGHT

Many inks which appear identical in ordinary light may appear very different when viewed under ultraviolet light or infrared radiation. Some inks may fluoresce under UV light, or simply appear to be different colours.

ACTIVITY 25

Testing with UV and IR light

Write out the word 'seven' on a piece of paper, using a pen with black ink. Using a different black pen add 'ty' to the word 'seven' in the same way that a forger might do. Now put the writing under an ultraviolet lamp. (**Remember:** *Never* look directly at a UV lamp.) Can you see any differences between the inks?

Now examine the writing under an infrared lamp. Make a note of your observations. Which gives the clearer results – the UV or IR lamp?

Though less common nowadays, it is possible to show where pencil has been *erased* (rubbed out) from a document using a rubber, by dusting the surface of the paper with a fluorescent powder. The particles of the powder stick to the traces of the rubber remaining on the surface, and can be observed clearly under the UV light.

However, changes to and erasures from paper documents are not only types of forgeries that the forensic scientist has to deal with. Many objects, such as cars, bicycles, keys, etc., have serial numbers stamped on them which could be used to identify them. With patient filing, a thief could remove the stamped number, and possibly even restamp the object if necessary with a different one. However, by treating the metal chemically, the forensic scientist can make the original number reappear!

Metals are made up of minute particles called *atoms*, arranged in a regular and orderly pattern.

Atoms in metal

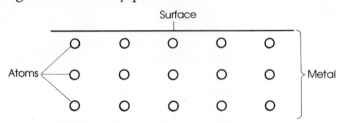

When a number is stamped on the metal, the layers of atoms below the stamp are compressed (squashed together).

The deformed surface

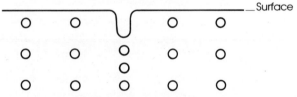

Even when the surface is filed or ground down flat, the compressed atoms remain compressed.

The compression remains, even after filing

By treating the surface with an acidic reagent which slowly dissolves the metal, the material which was smeared over the surface during filing is removed. Then the area of the surface which was punched will react with the acid faster than the surrounding area and an etched pattern will appear showing quite accurately the outline of the original marks.

Different metals require different etching reagents, but for mild steel alternate treatments with Fry's reagent (copper(II) chloride and hydrochloric acid solution) and nitric acid (about 20 per cent) for about a minute at a time generally brings quick results. Cast iron or steel, on the other hand, require treatment for many hours with a bichromate/sulphuric acid solution.

A redeveloped mark can normally be preserved by neutralising the acid, cleaning thoroughly, drying and then painting with a clear varnish, although, as always, it should be photographed if a permanent record is to be kept.

Testing marks on metal

Care! This activity involves the use of:
propanone (acetone) – *Flammable/irritant vapour/toxic!*
nitric acid $\Big\}$ *corrosive!*
Fry's reagent

Get someone to stamp a number, or numbers, on to a piece of mild steel, then file or grind down the surface until it is flat again. Don't ask what the number is: you are going to tell them!

1) Polish the surface of the metal with fine emery paper.

2) Carefully clean the surface of the metal with some propanone to remove any grease. Do not handle the surface again – either use gloves or hold the *edges* of the metal. (NB From a safety point of view, gloves are preferable since the reagents to be used are quite strong acids and are corrosive.)

3) Using tongs, dip some cotton wool into some Fry's reagent (9 g of copper(II) chloride dissolved in 12 cm^3 of concentrated hydrochloric acid and 10 cm^3 of water) and rub the surface of the metal for about a minute or so.

4) Dry the surface with some clean cotton wool then, using the tongs, dip some cotton wool into nitric acid (20% solution) and rub the metal surface for a further minute or so.

5) Dry the surface again with clean cotton wool.

6) Repeat steps 3), 4) and 5) until the original numbers stamped on the metal begin to appear. It may take only a few treatments, or you may have to go on repeating 3), 4) and 5) for up to half an hour – *be patient!*

7) Wash the metal in ammonia solution to neutralise any acid left on the surface and then dry with clean cotton wool. Put a thin coat of clear varnish over the numbers to help to preserve them.

NB   Cotton wool buds are ideal for this activity and using them is generally less awkward than rubbing the metal surface with cotton wool held in tongs!

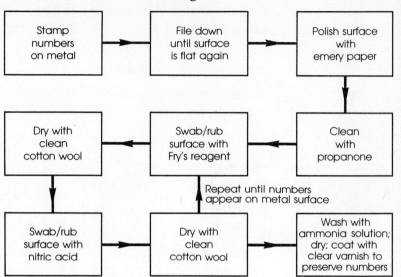

A method for testing marks on metal

QUESTIONS ON CHAPTER 10

1 Whilst entering a house at night, a thief knocked over a bottle of ink and spilled some on his clothes. He was later caught and forensic scientists compared the ink on his clothes with that remaining in the bottle.

(a) Three sets of apparatus were first made up, but each one had something wrong with it. Explain what is wrong with each diagram.

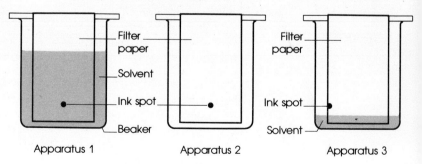

Various attempts to compare inks

(b) What is this method of analysis called?

(c) Having done the experiment correctly, the forensic scientist compared ink from the bottle, ink from some suspects' clothes and three pure inks.

These were one set of results:

The chromatogram

| Red | Blue | Green | Suspect | Bottle |

(i) How many inks were there in the suspect's sample?

(ii) What colours were in the suspect's sample?

(iii) Basing your decision on this evidence, was the suspect guilty or not guilty?

(d) The thief entered the room by breaking a window and then forcing the metal window frame with a screwdriver. As he climbed in, he cut his hand. Mention three other pieces of evidence that the police might look for.

2 The police sometimes offer to postcode your bicycle for you.

They do this by stamping your postcode on the frame of your bicycle so that it shows as an impression in the metal. Look at the diagram.

(a) Where would you look for your postcode if you wanted to know it?

(b) Why is your postcode useful if your bicycle is stolen?

(c) How could a thief remove the postcode?

(d) What could a forensic scientist use to show up the postcode after it had been removed by the method you have described?

(e) Using a small circle to represent an atom, draw a diagram to show how the atoms in a piece of metal are arranged.

(f) Draw another diagram to show how the position of the atom would be changed if the metal were struck by a sharp object like a chisel.

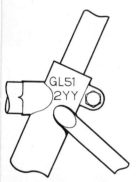

The police can stamp your postcode on the frame of your bicycle

3 (a) Which part of the spectrum might be used to compare drops of oil at the scene of the crime with oil from the suspect's car?

(b) Fluorescent pens are used by laundries to put an identification mark on customers' laundry. What is the advantage of using a fluorescent mark rather than an indelible ink mark?

85

SPECIALIST DEPARTMENTS

In addition to the three main departments of the forensic laboratory, i.e. the physical sciences, the biological sciences, and toxicology, there are several smaller specialist departments. Though smaller, they nevertheless play a vital role within the overall forensic service. By far the most important of these sections are the photographic unit and the firearms section.

THE PHOTOGRAPHIC UNIT

The photography unit generally provides a service to the rest of the laboratory. The work can involve photography in the ultraviolet, visible, and infrared regions of the spectrum, high speed photography, and many specialised techniques.

The department also deals with and reports on a number of cases where photographic evidence is required. Much of the work carried out by the 'forensic photographer' relies on his skill and experience, and vast amounts of sophisticated equipment are not normally necessary. The work, nevertheless, can be quite varied – maybe one day working for other departments, and perhaps the next day faced with the decision as to whether or not a negative originated from a particular camera, or asked to give an expert opinion on whether a photograph is a fake or not.

Photography is equally important, if not more so, to the police themselves, and each police force will have their own photographic departments. Photography as a method of keeping permanent records of evidence is vital to the police in many ways, for example: the scene of a crime or accident is photographed; fingerprints, when developed, are photographed; in addition to making casts of footprints, tyre marks, etc., photographs are also taken and, indeed, most of the comparison work is normally carried out using the photographs rather than the casts.

In fact, whenever visual evidence will need to be presented in court, and a permanent record kept in case of future appeals, photography is essential.

Consider the case of the burglar mentioned in Chapter 1. The footprints that he made in the flowerbed would have been photographed and then a cast made as well (as a precaution against the film in the camera being defective in some way). Photograph (a) below shows the burglar's shoeprint as found in the flowerbed. When the suspect was arrested, the soles of his shoes were photographed, as shown in photograph (b), and then an ink print was made of the patterned soles by pressing the shoes on to an ink pad, and then pressing them firmly on to clean white paper (photograph (c)).

The evidence of the footprint

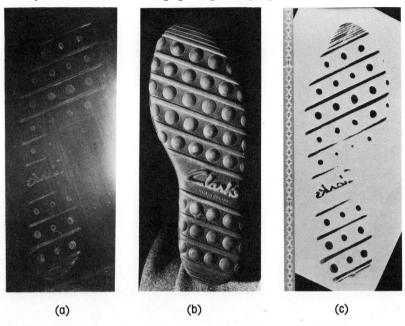

(a) (b) (c)

Photographs (a) and (c) are then carefully examined to find areas of similarity. In the same way that 16 points of similarity are required for positive identity when examining fingerprints, 16 points are also looked for here. Photographs (a) and (c) would then be labelled up, showing the 16 identical areas, as for matching fingerprints (p. 28).

On the photographs here, the 16 identical points on the sole patterns have *not* been marked up. Look for yourself; could you say with certainty that (a) and (c) were made by the same shoe?

THE FIREARMS SECTION

The firearms section of the forensic laboratory is growing in importance because of the increasing use of firearms in crime. Bullets from scenes of crimes, or from the unfortunate victim, are sent to the laboratory for an expert opinion as to the type of gun that fired them. If the gun itself is available, they may be asked to prove that the bullets were fired from that particular gun. In order to establish whether a bullet has come from a specific gun, the forensic scientist would use a 'shooting box' which enables him or her to shoot the gun and recover the test bullet undamaged. The test bullet and the bullet from the scene of the crime can be examined under the *comparison microscope* to observe any similarities.

But, what similarities are we looking for?

Guns generally have spiral grooves cut on the inside of the barrel. These grooves (or rifling, as it is called) cause the bullet to spin as it leaves the gun, enabling it to travel further and straighter.

A bullet is larger than the diameter of the barrel, but is made up of a soft metal on the outside which is scraped away as the bullet moves along. There has to be a tight fit in this way, otherwise the bullet would not be pushed out by the expanding gases. However, every gun has rifling marks that are unique, and an impression of these marks is left on the bullet as it moves along the barrel when the gun is fired. If a bullet from the scene of a crime is compared with a test bullet from the same gun, the rifling marks will be identical. Look carefully at the high magnification photograph shown below. It shows two bullets as seen under the comparison microscope. The uppermost bullet was involved in a crime and identified as coming from a .455 Webley Service revolver. The lower bullet in the photograph was fired from a gun of the same make and type, found in the possession of the suspect. Clearly, the bullets were fired from the same gun.

Bullets as seen under the comparison microscope

Other work that the firearms expert may be called upon to do includes such things as: testing shotguns to determine the spread of the shot at various ranges; giving an opinion as to the condition and functioning of guns that are submitted to him for examination; checking a bullet from the scene of a crime against bullets from previous unsolved crimes; examining cartridge cases (the marks left on a cartridge case by the firing pin are also unique to a particular gun), etc. To enable them to identify what type of gun a bullet was fired from, a firearms section would normally have a reference collection of different guns, bullets, etc., that could be used for visual comparison.

With the increasing use of firearms in crime in our modern society, the firearms section of the forensic laboratory is one that is likely to grow both in size and importance in the future.

QUESTIONS ON CHAPTER 11

1 Outline briefly the type of work that each of the following may be asked to do:
   (a) the photographic unit in the forensic laboratory,
   (b) the police photographic department.

2 (a) How can a firearms expert prove that a bullet has come from a particular gun?
   (b) What other tasks may the firearms expert be called upon to do?

WORDFINDER FOR SPECIALIST DEPARTMENTS

This time you are going to construct your *own* wordfinder. Draw a grid 12 squares by 12 squares. Looking back at the chapter, make up eight questions about the information given and write them down. Now write down the answers in the word square. Fill in the remaining squares with letters to hide your answers. Swap your wordfinder with someone else. Try to answer each other's questions and then look for the answers in the wordsquare!

INDEX

ELEMENTARY,
MY DEAR
WATSON!